PRAISE FOR *GRIEVING—THE SACRED ART*

"Lisa Irish shows us that grief is our ally in the Land of Loss, and indeed her book becomes our ally as well. Her insightful study and creative descriptions of grieving tap into our own experiences of loss. The roadmap is wise, but sensitive—grounded in hope—and reminds us to rest in God's healing love."
　　—**Richard Rohr, OFM**, The Center for Action
　　　and Contemplation

"There is a path from darkness into light. It is long and lonely. Lisa Irish has assembled a community of companions for this journey whose wisdom and whispers of encouragement lift the most broken among us. This book is a hand stretched out, an arm around the shoulder—it is tender, strong, reliable. Of all the books on grief, this is the one I would offer to a fellow soul on that bewildering journey through loss."
　　—**Jan Phillips**, author of *No Ordinary Time*

"A beautiful work of the heart. Lisa Irish speaks not only from a professional knowledge of loss, but from her own lived experience. Her exercises, meditations and rituals offer valuable counsel, and her understanding of the vulnerability of the journey is key. 'The heart initially begs for certainty,' she tells us, then goes on to show how the pathway through loss evolves, opening the door to a greater love that we may each find in our own way and time."
　　—**Paula D'Arcy**, author of *Gift of the Red Bird*
　　　and *Stars at Night*

"Grief and grieving are natural to life, but somehow we have convinced ourselves otherwise. Lisa Irish's *Grieving—The Sacred Art* returns us [to] the truth, and helps us navigate the sea of grief that we might arrive at the other shore with a greater appreciation for life and a greater boldness for living."
    —**Rabbi Rami**, author of *The World Wisdom Bible*

"Lisa Irish's approach to grieving in this volume invites the reader on a journey through the Land of Loss, through the regions of Alone, Passage, Surrender, and Changed. She shares in this context current research on grief and resilience, many evocative examples from her extensive experience in bereavement work and spiritual direction. Spiritual directors, pastoral counselors, chaplains, and the bereaved themselves are likely to better understand both the challenges and gifts of grieving. "
    —**Dr. Janet K. Ruffing, RSM**, Professor of the Practice of
    Spirituality and Ministerial Leadership, Yale Divinity
    School, New Haven, CT

"Armed only with the tools of psychiatry, I have found my ability to salve the wounds of grief often inadequate. Whether the bereaved is religiously minded or not, there is an inescapable, fundamentally spiritual aspect to grieving. Lisa Irish's *Grieving—The Sacred Art* compellingly speaks to this truth. But her missive does not flutter in the realm of imponderable metaphysics. Quotes from a variety of learned minds guide and inspire. Vignettes movingly illustrate the wisdom Ms. Irish shares. Her many entries headed "Promptings of Hope" offer practical help in navigating the Land of Loss to find hope."
    —**Joseph Fickes, MD**, Associate Director, Psychological
    Medicine Service, Yale New Haven Hospital

Grieving
—the sacred art

Hope in the Land of Loss

Lisa Irish

Walking Together, Finding the Way®

SKYLIGHT PATHS®
PUBLISHING
Nashville, Tennessee

SkyLight Paths Publishing
an imprint of Turner Publishing Company
Nashville, Tennessee
New York, New York
www.skylightpaths.com
www.turnerpublishing.com

Grieving—The Sacred Art: Hope in the Land of Lost

© 2018 by Lisa Irish

For information regarding permission to reprint material from this book, please write or fax your request to Turner Publishing, Permissions Department, at 4507 Charlotte Avenue, Nashville, Tennessee, (615) 255-2665, fax (615) 255-5081, or email your request to submissions@turnerpublishing.com.

Library of Congress Cataloging-in-Publication Data available upon request

10 9 8 7 6 5 4 3 2 1

Manufactured in the United States of America
Cover Design: Thor Goodrich
Interior Design: Tim Holtz

To my parents, Lillian and Ted,
who taught my heart how to love

CONTENTS

INTRODUCTION

She walked into my office, carrying her broken heart in trembling hands. I watched her sit down. She looked worn out from the burden of loss. Each breath, each sigh revealed her struggle with this new reality in her life. But here she was, asking for help. Somewhere in the swirl of painful and overwhelming emotions, she had hope that there was a way out. Or maybe it was desperation. It didn't matter. As her body crossed the threshold, she was taking an important step. Consciously or unconsciously, she said yes to the sacred journey of grieving.

Dear reader, you picked up this particular book on grief, and I'm so glad you did. It is my hope that you will find support here as you face the loss of your loved one. Our human relationships weave in and out of our lives, shaping us, teaching us, and, most of all, giving us the opportunity to love and be loved. The death of your mother or father, husband or wife, lover or dear friend, child or coworker, relative or neighbor sends ripples (or monsoons) into your heart and life. In this book you will learn grief's role in navigating the journey and test these ideas against your personal experience of loss. My number-one message to those I've helped with the grieving process is to honor your unique experience of grief. Respect it. Trust it. Your grief will lead you back to love.

If you are seeking help for another person, welcome. I think you'll find some insight here. I've combined personal and professional experience with current bereavement theory to describe loss and grief in an accessible way. My hope is to lift grief out of being identified as the *problem* to its correct distinction as the *solution*.

If you are like the woman with the broken heart, and you find yourself sinking into the painful, confusing experience of grief, please stay with me for a while. I honor your feelings. As we travel through these pages together, I invite you to listen to your heart and what it is telling you. There are many thoughts I will share here; some I have learned through my own journey of grief and others through my work supporting folks as they made their way through dark and lonely places. I offer these insights with a commitment to healing and an alliance with hope. Know that each stop along the way is written for you and your precious heart. Consider these ideas as you travel out of the darkness into the light. I trust your instincts and I encourage you to trust them as well.

BEGIN WITH COURAGE

It takes courage to seek help when you are grieving. It's hard to find that internal initiative to look at grief books or attend a support group when you are without energy or hope. So I'd like to say "Good for you" as you make these efforts for yourself. We live in a culture that is uncomfortable with death and subsequently with grief. Many employers offer only three days for bereavement; we may hear friends actually say, "You're not over that?" Grievers who ask for help find themselves a minority in a world that wants them to "move on."

As someone who is grieving, you have the basic right to attend to your feelings in the midst of your day-to-day life. For example, as outlined in grief counselor and educator Alan Wolfelt's "Mourner's Bill of Rights," you have the right to talk about your grief; you have the right to treasure your memories;

and you have the right to be tolerant of your physical and emotional limits.[1] In spite of our society's impatience with the grieving process, you do have and need the right to grieve. So if someone says to you, "It's time to get over it," you have permission to say, "I'm never going to get over it; I'm never going to get around it or under it. I have to go through it." Speaking this sort of truth guides those around you on how they can help you. When you explain, "I have to go through it," you invite friends to respect your unique process. In addition, each time you admit to yourself and to another that this normal human experience requires—even deserves—attention, you nurture your own courage to keep going. Courage is important here in the Land of Loss, as you travel the many twists and turns that come your way.

CONSCIOUS GRIEVING

Loss and grief weave into our lives as the seasons pass, as plans are made, as love is shared. Yet we still have a lot to learn about—and from—this painful human experience. Most of our learning takes place in the midst of unrelenting sadness, at a time when we have one goal: stop the pain. Grief is a time of emptiness and searching. We might seek help, but most people rely on traditions—both visible and invisible—from childhood homes. Many find themselves "going through the motions." The patterns from our childhood become the template for our grieving.

An alternative to this somewhat unconscious style of grieving is to enter the process as a participant. The waves of loneliness and confusion will continue to crash for a time. But as a conscious griever, you step into the sadness with more awareness, more tools, and perhaps more hope. Like an artist, a conscious griever makes choices that come from deep within, inviting grief to reveal the healing gift of that particular loss. Grieving consciously creates pathways into deeper self-knowledge, invites an increased ability to be grateful, and encourages connections to loved ones that transcend time and space.

I hope to encourage you to become aware of your own process of grieving. Take the time to observe your feelings and behaviors. Use the information, insights, and practical exercises to take care of yourself and your needs in this challenging time. Be gentle with yourself, especially in the choices you make. Conscious grieving respects both the hard work of grief and your tender heart, where grief resides. Conscious grieving becomes an opportunity for ongoing reflection, guiding you toward healing and hope.

ACCEPT YOUR UNIQUE EXPERIENCE

Everyone has experienced loss, but conscious grieving invites you to accept that loss and engage in a personal process of healing. Many seek help to speed things along, but unfortunately there is no singular formula or recipe. The journey moves as it will, based on your personality, your history and family culture, the circumstances around the death itself, financial or family pressures, and many other factors. These elements shape each individual's journey, creating their own timing and trajectory.

Grieving in our own unique way can also impact relationships. Well-meaning friends and family might offer support that is influenced by their experiences of loss or, more commonly, their discomfort with sadness. Differences and sometimes tensions may arise. In taking the first steps of conscious grieving, you are aware of the very personal and often lonely experience of grief. This new layer of awareness may also invite an inner strength that can guide the process. This is important. As you accept your unique experience of loss and learn to care for it, I hope you'll join me in trusting your inner life and in believing that conscious grieving will help heal the wounds of loss.

LET HOPE BE YOUR COMPANION

Accepting the responsibility for your own conscious grieving process intensifies another theme of this inner pilgrimage: our ultimate aloneness. We are forced to glimpse an existential truth of our humanity. The death of a loved one brings us right to the edge of this awareness as we search and search for their presence and find, instead, ourselves. That is where we begin, in the new, somewhat terrifying landscape of "me."

As you explore this new horizon, I invite you to join me in letting hope guide and support you. During our time together, consider the idea of hope as a source of healing. Open your heart to trusting the good in life and in others. Envision hope wrapping itself around your life and providing a bit of safety, a refuge, as together we bravely go forward into the depths of grief. In that dark place, let hope offer a comforting light as you make your way through. Grief is a built-in response to loss and will lead you in your healing.

The ideas that I offer throughout this book are intended to support you on your journey. Some are described as "experiments"; others are examples of self-care; others are aptly called "Promptings of Hope." Consider these suggestions as spiritual practices, resources, or homework to integrate the ideas in this book into your life. I invite you to imagine hope's light as it weaves its way through your story. Try on some of these ideas; let hope take root in your heart and shine on your path. With your participation, these practices and exercises will help you cultivate conscious grieving and will support your journey toward healing. With time you will return to that part of yourself that was lost when your loved one died. Let hope guide you and comfort you as you renew your connections with yourself and with your loved one.

THE LAND OF LOSS

When someone dies, we enter a new world: the Land of Loss. Suddenly, and without our consent, we must navigate this unknown terrain that coexists with the world around us. We may eat and sleep, go to work, and manage relationships and responsibilities, but our heart is often elsewhere. We live with an overwhelming sense of loss that causes us to peer out and wonder, "How is everyone else functioning?" We knew our role in the world we grew up in; we learned to make our bed or complete our education. Our heart learned about love and forgiveness and we saw the world as beautiful. We might even have felt loss before, but it didn't register in the same way. This time, loss pulled us into another reality with a completely new set of rules, most of them unknown. We look at ourselves in the mirror and see a stranger. We try to remember our loved one and experience instead a thick fog surrounding our heart and mind. In *Understanding Your Grief*, Alan Wolfelt describes it this way:

> Think of your grief as a wilderness—a vast, mountainous, inhospitable forest. You are in the wilderness now. You are in the midst of unfamiliar and often brutal surroundings. You are cold and tired. Yet you must journey through this wilderness. To find your way out, you must become acquainted with its terrain and learn to follow the sometimes hard-to-find trail that leads to healing.[2]

There are four regions in the Land of Loss: Alone, Passage, Surrender, and Changed. Each has its own landmarks, lessons to learn, and obstacles to confront. Each can become familiar and might slow down our travel; sometimes familiarity is easier to cope with than the confusion found in new areas of this strange and stark land. Or we might find ourselves going back and forth between regions, instead of taking a direct journey from entry to exit.

There is much to learn, but I hope you'll continue to trust me as a guide through this land. It will help you heal. Grief will help you find your way back to love.

While traveling through the four regions, we will learn about the "four tasks of mourning," described by J. William Worden in his book *Grief Counseling and Grief Therapy*. Grief is shaped by our unique approaches and feelings; we cannot package our experience into the same format as our neighbor or even our sibling. But there are some general tasks that we must address. Worden's foundational work in grief has spanned forty years and has become a fundamental resource to explain the process of grieving. For our purposes let's consider these four tasks as the mottoes of each region. Join me in this organic view of the process of grief and, as you read, try on the themes; let the stories connect with yours.

ALONE

Alone is the first region we encounter in the Land of Loss. It is here that we try "to accept the reality of the loss," as Worden says. Our deep sadness and feelings of loneliness lead us to the moment of realizing that "Nobody knows what I am going through . . . I am truly alone." Even if others knew our loved one, their grief is their own. In Alone, we confront our vulnerabilities and face a life without our loved one in it. Our primary resource in the Land of Loss is grief itself. And though unexpected land mines and traps appear along the way, grief is our constant ally and will guide us toward recovery.

PASSAGE

The confusing, constantly moving parts of grief are the central theme of Passage. For some, the experience of grief is like sinking into quicksand with a slow but sure pull into a frightening, even deadly, place. Others describe a catapult experience, a powerful thrust into the unknown. As we try to find our footing, memories of our loved one, childhood experiences, and normal human emotions all play a role in the impact of this loss. Questions about our own identity and the confusing response of people in our life add to the chaos.

Our task in Passage, Worden reminds us, is "to work through the pain of grief." Our heroic efforts take place within the context of all these moving parts, each trying to find their place in our story. We learn to hold on tight when the ride demands it, or, with practice, we might lean in to the next bend in the road. Moments of resilience and conscious grieving build our confidence and wisdom in the midst of the confusion. As we create our own map in the Land of Loss, hope is visible on the path, sometimes just enough for a single step, but always there, always available.

SURRENDER

Surrender is a place of deep change, as we accept life without our loved one in it. It is stepping off Cliffs of Uncertainty, "adjusting to a new world," as Worden tells us. As we walk through this profound transition, we learn to be gentle when we've always been strong, and brave when we've always been afraid. All the hard work in Passage lays the groundwork for the sacred terrain of Surrender, where we face the fear and powerlessness of loss. We learn that grief is not a journey toward accomplishment or a project to fix what is broken. We are invited to trust that healing will unfold as we ourselves unfold and let go into love. The sacred art of grieving calls us to a mystery far beyond ourselves, sometimes without words of comprehension, but always with the underlying strength of hope.

CHANGED

Changed offers a vision of transformation. We see a new horizon before us, calling us to the Land of Hope. Our journey has helped us redefine who we are and led us into a deeper relationship with ourselves, with our soul. Grief-work, such as practices of gratitude or ritual, sustains this life-giving, sacred connection and supports our relationship with our loved one and the Divine. Worden's final task, "to find an enduring connection with the deceased while moving forward with life" seems possible in Changed. We reweave our relationship with braids of love and treasure the bond that extends beyond death. We no longer fear the change that death demands; instead we learn to nourish our transformed soul and live life with a full heart.

MAY I INTRODUCE MYSELF?

I hope you feel the warmth I seek to offer throughout these pages. I am very familiar with the Land of Loss and know that a loving presence can make all the difference in the process. I hope you'll engage these words and the energy behind them as additional sources of comfort during your healing. My understanding of pain is both personal and professional. I offer you my utmost respect for seeking help.

My studies in education, theology, pastoral care, and spirituality, as well as my personal experiences, have prepared me to share this particular vision of loss and grief. I hope you will consider creating your own language of how loss changes us and how grief heals us as you make your way. Until then, feel free to borrow and work with the images and stories in this book. They are written with you in mind. As chaplain and bereavement coordinator for the Hospital of Saint Raphael and Yale New Haven Hospital in New Haven, Connecticut, I learned a lot about grief. I sat with individuals and groups for many hours, listening to their experiences of confusion, pain, loneliness, anger, and deep sadness. Immersed in the pain that claimed their hearts, my clients struggled to return to their lives. Relationships, work, health—all were influenced by the needs of their grieving hearts.

I found myself creating a safe place for tears. As these relationships grew, so did my clients' ability to grieve more consciously. I listened and helped identify landmarks and signposts along the way. Our relationship gave courageous women and men the permission to trust their experience and learn from it.

Grief's process of healing is indeed a sacred art. It calls to the deepest part of ourselves, touching long-forgotten places. Grief often stirs up our relationship with the Divine as well and invites us to ask if we believe, what we believe, and why we believe. The pilgrimage into our inner landscape, while forced upon us by the death of a loved one, can become a great lesson in love and in the Love that surrounds us all.

Two pictures hang in my writing room, one from an Irish castle and the other a Santa Fe cave dwelling. Both pictures are taken from inside the dark space, looking out into the light and landscape. They are my "diplomas" for this work. Yes, I have traditional diplomas, but the real training has been walking my own path of grief . . . sitting in the darkness of the cave and trusting the light before me. My losses include my mother's near-death in a car accident when I was two, leaving her a paraplegic, my father's death when I was eleven, and my mother's death when I was twenty-five.

This series of losses seemed to shape my life and my life's work as I sought understanding and healing. Thankfully

I have been graced with dear family and friends, skilled practitioners, and the tender presence of God throughout my journey. My professional roles have included teacher, adjunct professor, consultant, public speaker, campus minister, chaplain in long-term and acute care and bereavement settings, retreat leader, and spiritual director. In each I shared the wisdom I had at the time while supporting others in the discovery of their own inner light. I have faith in the evolving beauty of each person and in the ongoing presence of a God who loves without condition. It is in this spirit, the spirit of ministry, that this book is written to offer hope for the journey.

ONE MORE THOUGHT

Twentieth-century poet Rainer Maria Rilke's "Let This Darkness Be a Bell Tower" speaks to moments of grief. I invite you to sit with this sonnet as you prepare to join me in learning more about the sacred art of grieving. You are the "quiet friend" he greets. You have indeed "come so far" in your pain and darkness, as you open yourself to new ideas and to hope. See yourself as the bell that is battered and yet still sways and rings true. Trust your inner wisdom, leading you home—to your place in this world, to your gifts, to your capacity to love. Let hope light your way.

> *Quiet friend who has come so far,*
> *feel how your breathing makes more space around you.*
> *Let this darkness be a bell tower*
> *and you the bell. As you ring,*
>
> *what batters you becomes your strength.*
> *Move back and forth into the change.*
> *What is it like, such intensity of pain?*
> *If the drink is bitter, turn yourself to wine.*

In this uncontainable night,
be the mystery at the crossroads of your senses,
the meaning discovered there.

And if the world has ceased to hear you,
say to the silent earth: I flow.
To the rushing water, speak: I am.[3]

—Lisa Irish
Lake Beseck
Connecticut

PART 1

Alone

Still water rests against the outside edge of the Well of Sadness, a reflective pool that barely moves. No one knows how deep the well is; the tears of many travelers add to its ancient depths. Some stand for long periods of time, unable to move, unable to feel anything but sadness. The well holds their loss in its waters, almost protectively, and asks nothing in return. Each traveler encounters the Well of Sadness as their grief guides them, a fundamental experience in the Land of Loss.

The stark reality is inescapable. The disorientation is dizzying—nauseating for some, overwhelming for many. Regardless of the circumstances that led to this moment, we are not prepared for the cold truth of death and the resulting anguish of loss. We may have been here before, but *this* arrival in Alone is a unique event. Folks might come forward offering their support, but we must survive alone. The initial trauma of loss defines our disconnected experience in Alone, the entry point into the Land of Loss.

This sense of isolation within the shared human experience of loss reflects the theme of Alone. Advice and support may be all around us, but our individual emotions, history, and stories shape what loss feels like for each of us. Loss and grief may be universal, but at the same time, they are uniquely personal. Psychologist and emotions expert George Bonanno states,

> One of the most consistent findings is that bereavement is not a one-dimensional experience. It's not the same for everyone and there do not appear to be specific stages that everyone must go through. Rather, bereaved people show different patterns or trajectories of grief reactions across time.[1]

To move through Alone, then, we learn to work with our grief as a resource for healing. Grief is our ally, guiding us through acceptance, difficult challenges, and the tenderness of our feelings. Bonanno adds,

> We may be shocked, even wounded, by a loss, but we still manage to regain our equilibrium and move on. That there is anguish and sadness during bereavement cannot be denied. But there is much more. Above all, it is a human experience. It is something we are wired for, and it is certainly not meant to overwhelm us.[2]

Sometimes, though, it feels as if guilt or anger will indeed overwhelm us. Sometimes we stand before the Well of Sadness, unable to move, our hearts heavy with despair. The territory of Alone includes many painful—even dark—moments, but at the same time it provides glimmers of hope. We see new pathways that lead to life-giving choices; we name the sources of love and support that sustain us on the road. We open our hearts to the idea that our sadness need not supplant our hope; both can coexist in our grief and in our lives. Alone, while frightening at first, has much to teach us, as it prepares us for the rest of the journey. Take it one step at a time and trust the path before you.

CHAPTER 1

ENTERING LOSS

Your loved one is gone. The loss may feel incomprehensible, but the funeral and sympathy cards refuse to let you pretend otherwise. Every morning brings fresh pain; each sunrise is a reminder of death, not life. In the midst of missing this one special person, emptiness and disorientation fill any view of the future. And yet you must function—go to work, take care of others, breathe. Sometimes you survive through an autopilot response to this new, unwanted life. Alone, the entry into the Land of Loss, casts you into an emotional numbness that challenges your sense of self and your approach to life. This is normal, though it can be frightening. As counselor and teacher John E. Welshons describes, "The feelings are too overwhelming, too big. We fear we can't contain them all. So we turn them off."[1]

As you begin your trek, you are wrestling with the profound acknowledgment of what has happened and the resulting vulnerability that such change creates. As Welshons continues, "The numbness is a natural process. It is similar to the state of shock our body goes into after a serious physical trauma."[2] Be assured that all who have traveled this path have encountered some of what you are feeling, for there are common responses to loss. At the same time, your unique story will shape your personal sojourn through loss. In your aloneness, let yourself find comfort in the experiences of others, but also attend to the needs of your own heart, your own story. Let grief be your guide in this new Land of Loss.

ACCEPTING THE REALITY OF LOSS

Lauren's son, Ed, was driving to work in a faraway state. He parked on the side of the road to call his sister on her birthday. After laughing with and singing to his younger sibling, he said, "Uh-oh." Those were his last words. An eighteen-wheeler lost control on that same road, slamming into and through Ed's car.

Lauren's body convulsed with sobs as she recounted the story. Her tears seemed to have no end. Even as she told the tragic story of Ed's death, she couldn't truly accept what she heard herself saying. Every instinct screamed, "No! This can't be true!" Somehow Lauren had managed all the details around her son's death. Still, her broken heart needed more time and care to comprehend her experience of loss.

How can anyone cope with a loss like this? The trauma of loss slams into every aspect of our lives: physical, emotional, spiritual, and intellectual. Yet society expects that we will continue to function, take care of others, and keep going. For many of us, it is as if we live two lives: one where we meet our social responsibilities and expectations; the other in the lonely realm of loss, where we experience everything through the lens of sadness. It is here, in the deepest places of our hearts, that we begin the painful and unavoidable journey of grieving.

J. William Worden's first task of mourning is "to accept the reality of the loss."[3] This is an ongoing task in the territory of Alone, guiding us on the path toward healing. Acceptance is not always easy to do. Despite all the facts before us, we may cling to a lingering disbelief that controls how much truth we let in or how many feelings we are willing to experience. Worden explains, "Coming to an acceptance of the reality of loss takes time since it involves not only intellectual acceptance but also an emotional one."[4] Our natural response is to avoid and protect ourselves from pain. Grief assists with the delicate process of removing layers of denial and disbelief, easing us toward a path of healing.

As novelist Joan Didion described in her best-selling memoir *The Year of Magical Thinking*, she experienced the shelter of denial after the death of her husband, Gregory. Despite being with her husband when he suffered his fatal heart attack in their home, making her way through the mourning rituals, and even managing to dispose of some of his clothes, Didion couldn't let go of her husband's slippers.

> We might expect if the death is sudden to feel shock. We do not expect this shock to be obliterative, dislocating to both body and mind. We might expect that we will be prostrate, inconsolable, crazy with loss. We do not expect to be literally crazy, cool customers who believe their husband is about to return and need his shoes.[5]

A similar experience happened to author Barbara Lazear Ascher, traveling in the landscape of Alone four years after the death of her husband from pancreatic cancer. During an appointment, her internist, who noticed how grief was taking a toll on Ascher's physical health, frankly said, "Bob is not coming back." Ascher knew this—deep down—but on some level still didn't believe it:

> I hadn't realized the power of denial, grief's strongman. Nobody knows she's in denial; that's what denial is. . . .

I hadn't known I thought Bob was coming back after all this time. I hadn't known I was keeping everything, including my heart, ready for his return. Just in case.[6]

Our creative unconscious initially protects us through such forms of denial. They serve a valuable purpose, protecting us from the painful trauma of loss. The numbness moves into a disbelief until we're ready to grasp the truth. Eventually yielding to a process of acceptance, those layers of protection become layers of awareness. Events, seasons, or time itself allow the protective layers to open up and our awareness shifts: You return to the nursing home where your mother died; you receive a newsletter from your spouse's nature club; you turn the page of the calendar to your friend's birthday month; you crave your dad's special cookies at Christmastime. Each reminder allows the truth to sink in just a little more. Emotions will follow, some like waves that threaten your ability to stay standing. Slowly, your reality is transformed and the grip of denial is loosened. The pain of loss seeps in as your heart acknowledges the truth. With your participation, healing begins its deep and rhythmic journey.

By accepting the reality of our loss, we are not being asked to approve of it. Rather, our acceptance is acknowledgment that loss happened, life has changed, and adaptation has begun. This experience cannot be rushed. There is no time line for grief. Your unique story, your loved one, and your own needs combine to create a specific path for your healing. This path through loss evolves with your acceptance and participation, but the timing and rhythm have a life of their own. "The pressures for people to get over grief . . . seem to be based on a very simplistic view of what loss is," grief researcher Paul Rosenblatt reports. With time you learn that "loss is often a series of losses or of realizations."[7]

We are traveling into deeper awareness as "sorrow carves riverbeds in our souls, deepening us as it flows in and out of our lives," notes psychotherapist Francis Weller.[8] This is the premise surrounding the Land of Loss. Grief, in helping us adapt to the inevitable changes, is leading us back into ourselves and, ultimately, back into love. Weller writes, "Sorrow is a sustained note in the song of being alive. To be human is to know loss in its many forms. This should not be seen as a depressing truth. Acknowledging this reality enables us to find our way into the grace that lies hidden in sorrow."[9]

Promptings of Hope

Emily Dickinson writes that hope "sings the tune without the words, and never stops at all." It helps to practice being hopeful, just as you might practice an instrument, a foreign language, or a yoga pose. Experiment with one or all of these explorations into hope.

Begin by getting comfortable with hope in less critical sides of life. For example, the next time you are in a traffic jam, remind yourself that this problem will ultimately resolve itself and you *will* be moving again soon. If it helps, focus on your breath. Slow it down; inhale through your nose and exhale through your mouth. Tell yourself, "It's *okay*. I choose hope, and this will be *okay*." Let hope grow in small, resolvable situations.

Or in quiet moments write down the name of someone you consider to be a hopeful person. Jot down examples of his or her hopefulness. Look on this list and wonder, "What would it feel like to carry hope in my heart?" Then, if you can, experiment with feeling hopeful—even if only for a minute or two. Visualize hope as an imaginary jacket; slip your arms into it and see what it feels like.

You can also create a personal symbol of hope—a special stone, a piece of jewelry—and carry it with you throughout your day. Take a moment to say a blessing, prayer or intention over this symbol, asking in your deepest places that hope be renewed when you look at or hold this symbol. Invite hope to comfort and support you on your journey of grief. Let it become part of your healing.

TRUST YOUR VULNERABILITY

The journey into the Land of Loss brings us face-to-face with a most tender part of who we are—our vulnerability. We feel disoriented as the self we thought we knew gets lost in the chaos and unpredictability of our grief. For some of us, grief becomes like life inside a pinball machine, with our emotions erratically kicking us from side to side. We are bounced without warning from one feeling to the next. Others of us will be immobilized by these strong emotions, as if mired in a frozen sludge of feelings. Much of our energy is used just to breathe. The confusing demands of grief take over, our sense of self is diminished, and we are left with vulnerability in its place.

In her memoir of her brother's death from AIDS at age thirty-one, Barbara Lazear Ascher presents her experience of grief as a "landscape without gravity," an apt description for this lonely, vulnerable place.[10] Emotions float all around, one indistinguishable from another. Responsibilities and expectations hover nearby, but it is impossible to hold on to anything. Regardless of how we describe the early grief experience, loss intensifies a basic truth of our existence: We come into and we leave this world alone. We are powerless to change this reality.

After his wife died in a car accident, Tom admitted feeling lonely in a world of couples. Everywhere he looked he saw people traveling two by two, and he did not have a partner. Life lost its purpose for Tom. He made choices each day, but Tom still felt adrift and isolated. He kept going, as in "going through the motions." Friends commented on how well he was doing. But deep inside, or when he looked in the mirror, he knew it was an act. His wife was gone, but it felt as if something else was gone as well. In his grief, Tom felt helpless, defenseless, exposed. He felt vulnerable.

Tom chose to ask for help to explore his feelings, but many of us avoid our vulnerability. We keep busy to numb the ever-present feelings of helplessness. We seek certainty where it does not exist. Death has taken our loved one and it feels as if grief is trying to take our identity as well. We resist the process, asking, "What am I doing wrong? How can I get better? Why am I so weak?" We believe that "staying strong" will protect us from the pain of loss. But our vulnerability is distinct from grief's emotional ride. Vulnerability is not weakness, but rather a part of our humanity. To heal, we learn to trust the tender place inside that has no answers.

As Brené Brown, research professor at the University of Houston Graduate College of Social Work, reminds us, "The perception that vulnerability is weakness is the most widely accepted myth about vulnerability *and* the most dangerous." [11] She goes on to explain, "If we want to reclaim the essential emotional part of our lives and reignite purpose and passion, we have to learn how to own and engage with our vulnerability and learn how to feel the emotions that come with it." [12]

Grief and its myriad emotional demands guides us toward a new understanding of our vulnerability. When you experience feelings of powerlessness, you may initially resist them. Instead, trust your vulnerability to help you travel through Alone. The more you understand about yourself, the better able you are to align yourself with the healing process. We anchor our feelings when we name and acknowledge them. Once tethered, we can live with our emotions, as painful as they are, and listen for the wisdom they offer. Thirteenth-century Persian poet Rumi explains:

> *This being human is a guest house*
> *Every morning a new arrival.*
>
> *A joy, a depression, a meanness,*
> *some momentary awareness comes*
> *as an unexpected visitor.*
>
> *Welcome and entertain them all!*
> *Even if they are a crowd of sorrows,*
> *who violently sweep your house*
> *empty of its furniture,*
> *still treat each guest honorably.*
> *He may be clearing you out for some new delight.*
>
> *The dark thought, the shame, the malice,*
> *meet them at the door laughing,*
> *and invite them in.*
>
> *Be grateful for whoever comes,*
> *because each has been sent*
> *as a guide from beyond.*[13]

Our vulnerability is not a trap or hazard in our loss, but rather a secret passageway that leads to a strong, beautiful heart. For, in addition to holding the raw and wild emotions that come with loss, Brown says, "Vulnerability is the birthplace of love, belonging, joy, courage, empathy, and creativity. It is the source of hope, empathy, accountability, and authenticity."[14] Accept all the feelings, difficult and supportive alike. Each are part of your journey and your healing. Let the wisdom found in your vulnerability guide your choices in grief. As noted grief counselor and educator Thomas Attig comments, "Although bereavement happens to us, grieving is what we do in response to it. Far from being choiceless, our coping is pervaded by choice."[15]

Promptings of Hope

Lin Yutang, author of *The Importance of Living*, tells us, "Hope is like a road in the country; there was never a road, but when many people walk on it, the road comes into existence." This is where we begin in the Land of Loss. Hope reveals itself when we rely upon it. With every step we take, we etch the path of hope into our lives. Develop an intentional relationship with hope and increase your capacity to see hope's presence along the way.

Self-expression will assist you in cultivating this relationship. Written, visual, physical, musical, verbal—all forms of expression provide release for painful feelings and access to healing and hope. You do not need lessons or permission to give voice to what is inside you. Write in a journal, doodle in the margins of a novel, cry along with the radio. Creative expression, a natural human quality, can assist you in making sense of your new world. Whether you write a poem, scribble abstract shapes, or sigh in the shower, your self-expression will help you identify your feelings and move closer to your vulnerable heart. Choose one and start.

COMMONALITIES OF GRIEF

While we each have our own unique experience of grief, it can be comforting to know that we also share many of the human reactions to loss. That is the universal nature of grief. Naming some of these similarities can help us feel less alone and provide a map of possible stops on the road ahead. Therese Rando, esteemed bereavement specialist and author, describes aspects of grief that are part of our common human experience:

Grief is not just sadness or depression. It is a whole host of emotions ranging from anxiety to anger to guilt to confusion to relief and more. Besides affecting your emotions, it reaches into every part of your life, touching your work, your relationships with others, and your image of yourself. . . . You can expect grief to have an effect on you psychologically, socially, and physically.[16]

Later we will discuss the variety of factors that create unique configurations of individual responses to loss. For now, here are some common reactions to guide you and your understanding of grief.

LONGING, LACKING FOCUS, LOSING CONTROL

We know that broad and swift emotional swings are a natural response to loss. For some, grief is a portal into new feelings that are frightening, or a trigger for old feelings that have been tucked away, their pain carefully forgotten. Sadness, guilt, and loneliness are expected, but it is interesting to learn how common it is to yearn for our loved one. A 2000–2003 study found yearning to be the defining feature of grief and an emotion that most clearly reflects the absence of the deceased:

Yearning is a longing for reunion with the deceased loved one, heartache about an inability to reconnect with this person. Individuals may cognitively accept the death of a loved one, but they may still pine for them and experience pangs of grief (i.e., yearning).[17]

The elastic band of yearning attaches to many of us when we arrive in Alone, keeping us bound to the emptiness caused by loss. We can't move forward without absence pulling us back into pain. Our longing generates an undeniable and primal experience that may be possible to name, but can be impossible to see beyond. This common response adds to the anguish of grief. For some, the longing itself becomes a replacement for what has been lost. Patience and self-compassion are necessary to navigate the challenging experience of yearning. Thomas Attig writes, our journey will teach us how to "make a transition from caring about others who are present to caring about them when they are absent."[18] With grief's assistance our longing will teach us about the love that is with us always.

It's also normal to wrestle with lack of focus and energy. You discover that you started the washer without any clothes in it; you forget an appointment you made just yesterday; or you can't find the motivation to get to the gym. The energy and concentration required to cope with everyday life is just not available while you are living in the Land of Loss. You are simply too overwhelmed with its emotional demands. Some may fear that these behaviors are signs of going crazy, but they are not. Alan Wolfelt suggests, "Be on the lookout for the trail marker that affirms your sanity: Recognize You Are Not Crazy. It's an important trail marker, because if you miss it, your entire journey through the wilderness of your grief may feel like Alice's surreal visit to Wonderland."[19]

Instead of questioning your sanity, learn to be kind to yourself. Your world has turned upside down; who wouldn't get confused once in a while? Learn to treat yourself as you would treat a neighbor who has had a loss: be patient, generous, supportive, and loving.

In addition to longing and lacking focus, many of us experience a sudden loss of emotional control. This rush of deep emotion is a normal response, and is known as a STUG. Coined by Therese Rando, STUG stands for sudden (or subsequent) temporary upsurge of grief, which describes the familiar "out-of-control" experiences that many of us encounter.

Some folks proclaim, "I've been STUGged!" to explain the intense, surprising waves of emotions. These powerful feelings happen without warning, last for varying lengths of time, and can feel like ocean swells of pain coming from deep within. You may be blindsided by a STUG when you are walking down the cereal aisle in the grocery store. There on the shelf you see your spouse's favorite cereal, and you start crying uncontrollably. A STUG could appear as an ache that takes hold out of nowhere at your niece's wedding and builds into a sob, right there in front of everyone.

A STUG is a release of pent-up grief, a kind of a pressure-cooker response to your loss. It's a crack in your control as you try to function normally. It is your heart reminding you of your deep connection to your loved one who has died, however embarrassing this surprising display may be for you. STUGs teach us that our feelings are complex. They can't be managed like a budget or structured like a recipe. Our feelings, and all that is attached to them, sometimes express themselves without our permission—in the case of grief, that is okay.

RELATIONSHIPS ALONG THE WAY

We live with and among other people. Our relationships will be affected by our grief, which is now part of who we are. For example, restlessness and irritability, both normal aspects of grief, sometimes find their way into relationships. You might be unable to sit still and listen to a story, and then feel guilty that you aren't being a good friend. On another day, your sister's stories are just too painful to hear; they remind you of what has been lost, so you avoid contact altogether. Light-hearted conversations or gossip about the neighbors can become tedious and then you feel impatient with friends and family. You might feel as if your kindness and affection for others has turned into a short fuse, a lack of tolerance. Loss and grief have rearranged your worldview and it is going to take some time to get reoriented. Your generosity toward others will return, but this is the time to discover generosity toward yourself. Any social interaction—picnic, wedding, book group, work—may present new challenges in relationships. Your energy and needs deserve your attention and monitoring as you go along. As Rando comments,

> If you lack the energy to be involved socially with others, you may find it easier to decline social offers than to accept them. On the other hand, you might behave in an opposite fashion and become excessively fearful, dependent, and clingy. You may try to avoid being alone and surround yourself with others to distract yourself. Sometimes you may hide your grief fearing that others will get sick of listening to you and then, they too, will leave you.[20]

In the Land of Loss, it's important to take time for yourself as you observe, build, rely upon, and change your relationships with others. Trust the path and the opportunities for self-care that appear. Time alone in an elevator, completing simple tasks, or wrapping up in a warm blanket or prayer shawl can become places of refuge as you move forward. The pace is yours to set.

GRIEF'S PHYSICAL TOLL

While some of us are more in touch with our bodies than others, the evidence is in: Our minds and bodies are linked. Just as a physical ailment will affect our emotions, grief's emotional upheaval will influence our physical health in some or all of the following ways:

- Being unable to sleep—or sleeping too much
- Indigestion, overeating, undereating
- Decrease in energy and motivation
- Chest pain, shortness of breath
- Nervousness, agitation
- Lump-in-the-throat feeling
- Loss of pleasure
- Lack of strength, exhaustion
- Feeling unsteady, dizzy
- Change in sexual desire

Broken hearts can be comforted by attentiveness to the body. As a conscious griever, your task is to pay attention to what your body is saying and then compassionately respond to its messages. Self-compassion, an intentional loving concern for oneself, is a valuable practice, and the body is a good place to start. If sleep is a problem, change your habits—try new nighttime or morning routines, or get more exercise so your body will appreciate its rest. Rearrange your bedroom or change the size and shape of your pillows. If your body is speaking to you through agitation or exhaustion, sit down and listen to it. Have a dialogue with your body and ask what it needs. Alan Wolfelt reminds us,

> Good self-care is important at this time. Your body is the house you live in. Just as your house requires care and maintenance to protect you from the outside elements, your body requires that you honor it and treat it with respect. The quality of your life ahead depends on how you take care of your body today.[21]

If you need extra support, go to your doctor or naturopath to share your concerns and receive suggestions. The more you take care of your body, the more its wisdom will help you heal.

THE SEARCH FOR MEANING

When death arrives, our emotional pain often intensifies our need to make sense of what has happened. We ask, "What could I have done to stop this?" or "How will I go on?" or simply, "Why?" We sift through our beliefs, family teachings, or the wisdom of others to comprehend our loss. There are often no satisfying answers, for death is a painful mystery. Some of us respond to death's mystery as victims, believing we have been wronged by God or the universe. Others turn to a faith tradition and find comfort in how that tradition responds to death. We rarely accept death as the mystery it is, for our attention is often on finding ways to lessen the pain of loss. Thomas Attig explores the idea that "As we encounter mysteries, we must learn and relearn to let go and resist the temptation of believing they are ultimately solvable, manageable, controllable, and manipulable."[22] While we can't always get clear-cut *answers* that will ease our pain, the *motivation* to make sense of our loss can become a source for healing.

Meaning-making helps us cope. Consider our reaction to the death of an elder after a long, happy life. We give meaning to their life and we are comforted in the midst of our sadness by the legacy they offered. The death of a firefighter mom or dad is eased with stories of heroism on the job. Through meaning-making we find clarity in our grief. In *Lessons of Loss: A Guide to Coping*, grief researcher, educator, and therapist Robert A. Neimeyer states, "Loss . . . requires us to reconstruct a world that again 'makes sense,' that restores a semblance of meaning, direction, and interpretability to a life forever transformed."[23] Our inherent search for meaning becomes a pathway for our grief. Neimeyer suggests that we view our life as a story and see ourselves as the author. "Like a novel that loses a central supporting character in a middle chapter, the life disrupted by bereavement forces its 'author' to envision potentially far-reaching changes in plot in order for the story to move forward in an intelligible fashion."[24] This image of the grief process invites us to take a hands-on approach to the continual revisions that life ends up asking of us. When we participate in this way, we accept that change and adaptation will continue to be a part of our story. Our intrinsic search for meaning supports healing through a creative, reflective response to our life.

Promptings of Hope

"Hope is being able to see that there is light despite all of the darkness," proclaims Archbishop Emeritus Desmond Tutu. Put his words into action and examine the effects of grief that you are currently experiencing.

Working in the center of a piece of paper, allowing for a two-inch margin on all four sides, write down the physical, spiritual, and psychological symptoms of your grief. Add columns, if you like, to keep them bunched together on the middle of the page. Write mindfully, perhaps remembering specific moments in your grief.

When you're done, draw a heart around what you've written. Let that heart bring light into your grief and into the very challenging journey before you. You can draw more than one heart or add words, such as *patience* or *trust*, as you consider your list. Offer yourself the compassion any grieving person needs and deserves.

CHAPTER 2

GATHERING YOUR RESOURCES

A rrival in the Land of Loss is daunting. It is important to pack up the gear you need for such a journey. What do you have around you, or within you, that might help? If your living situation is safe and secure, count that as a blessing and carry it with you. If you grew up with a variety of siblings who taught you how to roll with the punches, consider the strength you can draw from those memories. For some, faith is a rich resource. For others, curiosity will help you navigate this new terrain. There is always more to learn and more to add to a gratitude list.

It may surprise you to learn that grief itself is one of your resources in loss. Grief is your steadfast companion and will guide you well. You are traveling with a heart that begs for certainty, and what you will find is the invitation to live with ambiguity. Don't despair. As Francis Weller writes, we let our hearts remain open "in order to keep leaning into the world; to keep moving grief through our psyches and bodies, so we can taste the sweetness of life."[1] Learn how to embrace both sadness and hope on this sacred trek through Alone. You might think you have to choose one or the other, but you don't. Your resources include a nondual mind-set that embraces both and will support your growth and healing.

GRIEF IS OUR ALLY

As her mother was dying, Nancy was a devoted and compassionate caregiver. She used any available time to sit with her mom, sing to her, and hold her hand. After her mother's death, Nancy returned to her routine of work and family time, but her heart was always a few steps behind. She encountered regular reminders of her mother's absence; she was often moved to tears in the middle of a conversation. Nancy decided to see me to get help with her grief because she felt "it was clearly a problem" for her. She knew she was sad—she missed her mother. But this ongoing grief had to be managed, she explained impatiently, because it was too unpredictable and confusing.

My conversations with Nancy circled around the events, people, and feelings that were in her life while she coped with her mother's absence. Nancy extended compassion to her siblings to help them through the loss. As the office manager for a nonprofit organization, Nancy's work life was full and usually demanding. She was grateful for her husband's and adult children's presence in her life, and shared concern for their grief. But as she sat in my office, it became clear that she viewed her own grief as an interference in getting things back to normal.

Most people think grief is something to be endured or fixed. We attend support groups, for example, to help grief go away. We stay busy to push the feelings aside. The memories and deep feelings may call to us, but we're often too lonely or in too much pain to listen. When friends say, "Maybe it's time to move on," we are outraged. At the same time, we wonder, "Shouldn't I be doing better by now? How do I stop this grief?"

It is a common reaction to try to rush grief. For some, the pain is unendurable. For others, a constant ache influences daily life. We might feel pressure from those around us to "be strong" and, at the same time, feel weakened by our fears when we admit the depths of our sadness. Unfortunately, our desire to put grief behind us is encouraged by the psychiatric community, which assigns six months as the typical period of grieving and labels anything beyond that as "prolonged grief disorder."[2] But each loss is different and each experience of grief deserves assessment and attention. There are individuals whose needs require medical support, and "diagnosis is reserved for those for whom the benefits outweigh any potential harm. Such people are entitled to the care, compassion, and the privileges accorded to the sick by society."[3] For most of us, though, grief is a normal process and we would benefit from a generalized permission to just be sad when a loved one dies.

I seek to rearrange our relationship with grief. Instead of merely tolerating it, how can we embrace grief and its role in healing from loss? As our ally, grief replaces society's urging to move *on* with our heart's call to move *in*. Grief can be a curative. It assists the healing of our emotional pain in the same way our cells protect and organize the healing of a broken bone. The energy we expend to keep grief at arm's length hinders the process and often becomes partly responsible for our exhaustion. But when we accept grief as a resource to recover from loss, we tap into the fullness of our humanity and the emotional reserves that lie within each of us. We open new places in our heart as it stretches and grows. Dr. Thomas Attig, who teaches about loss and grief through the lens of philosophy, states:

> When we . . . are bereaved, our losses disrupt our ways of experiencing and living in the world that we have learned previously and come to take for granted. We

lose our bearings and feel at a loss as to how to go on. We have lost not only the presence of the one who has died but much of what we took for granted. Our losses shake our confidence in potentially everything else that we also took for granted. As we cope with losses through death, we relearn what remains trustworthy in what we took for granted; where our old ways are no longer viable, we learn new life patterns. As we relearn our ways in the worlds of our experience, we find new ways of going on in the absence of those who died, including new ways of living and being ourselves.[4]

As your ally, grief assists you in this arduous process of relearning the world. The timing and patterns of this relearning will change as you change. Your task is to stay aware of your needs and respond to them. Journalist Daniel Goleman reported, "[Grieving], when successful, removes one from the stream of life to ponder one's own place in the world and one's relationship with the dead person, and finally to return to that stream having adjusted to living with loss."[5] Grief will stay with you as long as it needs to, helping you sort out the changes that loss has created. It provides the space to step into memories and the tender feelings that follow. Grief offers a pathway to integrate your loved one into the life before you while treasuring the past you shared.

Promptings of Hope

Best-selling author Anne Wilson Schaef is often quoted as saying, "My grief and my pain are mine. I have earned them. They are a part of me. Only in feeling them do I open myself to the lessons they can teach." Consider *your* relationship with grief. When did you first encounter it in your lifetime? How old were you and what were your feelings? What were the circumstances of the loss and the reactions of the people around you? Look at other moments in your life when grief appeared. How do you feel about past experiences of grieving?

I encourage you to take some time to write a letter to your grief. Start with "Dear Grief," and just keep writing. If it helps, think of your grief as a relative you have mixed feelings about, perhaps a distant one or one that just won't move out. Tell grief about your feelings and fears. Challenge grief, if you wish, and ask questions that may not get answered. Take your time, and create a relationship with your grief that is open and honest.

KEEPING AN OPEN HEART

As her parents' health declined, Martha remained committed to caring for them. It was not easy. She worked with outside agencies to provide meal delivery and home health aides, in spite of her mother's consistent dissatisfaction with both. Martha drove her parents to all their appointments while working part time and managing other family commitments. Her mother's death came after months of hospitalizations and a stay at a local hospice. In the midst of her own sadness and grief, Martha shifted gears to keep track of her dad's emotional needs. She supported his process of reentering life after the death of his wife of sixty years, respecting his dignity and independence while sometimes ignoring her own physical and emotional needs. Worn out, Martha struggled as she cared for her elderly father. She knew loss would return once again, and she was unsure her heart could withstand the pain.

Our human capacity to love and be loved remains a mystery. We know what it feels like, but we often have a hard time describing the experience. We might agree, though, that love comes alive when our hearts are open. It is a challenge for many of us to keep our heart open after it has been deeply wounded by loss. This dynamic is complicated further when months or years of caregiving precede the death. We become worn out and overwhelmed by the practical and emotional demands that caring for another requires. Many people find it easier to shut down their feelings to protect themselves from the pain of loss. This defensive maneuver may provide temporary relief, but it also interferes with the grieving process. In many situations our grief is delayed or extended in response to efforts to close off our hearts. Alan Wolfelt reminds us: "You will learn over time that the pain of your grief will keep trying to get your attention until you have the courage to gently, and in small doses, open to its presence. The alternative—denying or suppressing your pain—is in fact more painful."[6]

It is no wonder we cast grief as the enemy in our experience of loss. Over and over we are reminded of our loved one's absence; over and over we feel sadness, loneliness, or despair. Grief's insistence becomes our heartbreak, so a closed heart becomes our protection. But as Wolfelt goes on to explain, our attempt to protect ourselves becomes a denial of ourselves, and that does not lead us toward healing or return us to love:

> I have learned that the pain that surrounds the closed heart of grief is the pain of living against yourself, the pain of denying how the loss changes you, the pain of feeling alone and isolated—unable to openly mourn, unable to love and be loved by those around you. Instead of dying, while you are alive, you can choose to allow yourself to remain open to the pain, which in part, honors the love you feel for the person who has died.[7]

An open heart is a precious resource. It cannot be underestimated and usually requires extra care. When we nourish our heart in creative and contemplative ways, it will continue to speak to us. Our role as conscious grievers is to listen for its wisdom. If a line of poetry or an email message touches you, stop for a moment and receive the insight. If you watch the birds in winter and find their perseverance inspiring, wait a minute. Watch the scene just a little longer . . . birds flying among the white specks, landing on the snow-frosted suet . . . how does this touch your heart? If a memory or a line of music creates deep sadness and tears return, savor the feelings that follow. Remember, love's seed was planted in your heart and grows there alongside your loss. Francis Weller writes, "It is grief, however, that allows the heart to stay open to this love, to remember sweetly the ways these people touched our lives. It is only when we deny grief's entry into our lives that we begin to compress the breadth of our emotional experience and live shallowly."[8]

How do you return to love after your heart has been broken by loss? The real question is, how do you not? We are made to love; our grief is a testament to a gift of love that we have received. Step forward into your feelings and remember that a heart closed to pain becomes a heart closed to love. Unitarian minister Arthur Powell Davies tells us that with an open heart, even our anguish can be part of our healing:

> When sorrow comes, let us accept it simply, as part of life. Let the heart be open to pain, let it be stretched by it. All the evidence we have says this is the better way. An open heart never grows bitter. Or if it does, it cannot remain so. In the desolate hour, there is an outcry; a clenching of the hands upon emptiness; a burning pain of bereavement; a weary ache of loss.
>
> But anguish, too, is a door to life. Here, also, is a deepening of meaning—and it can lead to dedication; a

going forward to the triumph of the soul, the conquering of the wilderness. And in the process will come a deepening inward knowledge that in the final reckoning, all is well.[9]

Promptings of Hope

Jack Kornfield, leading Buddhist mindfulness practitioner, tells us in "A Meditation on Grief": "It takes courage to grieve, to honor the pain we carry. . . . We need to respect our tears. Without a wise way to grieve, we can only soldier on, armored and unfeeling, but our hearts cannot learn and grow from the sorrows of the past." Contemplative practices, such as centering prayer, journaling, silent retreats, and deep listening, can support your wounded heart and help you create inner calm, reduce stress, and cultivate compassion—for yourself and others in your life. Books, CDs, classes, and online instruction are available resources. Until then, experiment with this centering exercise to experience a taste of inner quiet. Your grieving heart might find comfort in the calm of the present moment.

If possible, practice this exercise for five to ten minutes if you are new to contemplative practice, or longer if you are an experienced practitioner of mindfulness.

To prepare:

- Read through the exercise before you start. Give yourself permission to follow the steps without the pressure of being perfect. You're trying something out; just see how it feels. Sit in a comfortable and private place. Meditative music and silence are both helpful as you seek to find your center. Breathe deeply to release tension before the exercise, then relax into normal breathing and proceed.

To begin:

- Close your eyes and imagine yourself sitting by a river. Take time to notice the sound of the flowing water, the sight of the green leaves and blue sky, the fresh air on your skin.

- Inhale deeply through your nostrils and imagine that you are breathing in the beauty around you.

- Exhale slowly through your mouth and imagine that you are breathing out your fears and concerns.

- Repeat the in-breath and out-breath, focusing on being present to this one moment.

- When your busy brain sends a thought or emotion that disrupts the quiet, imagine the distraction as a leaf floating by on the water. You see it, but you don't need to do anything about it. Let it float by, and return your focus to your quiet space beside the river.

- Breathe in, breathe out, be.

- You are safe, you are loved, you are here.

- When it is time to stop, do so slowly, almost reverently. If you are comfortable, offer a prayer of gratitude for the gift of quiet.

HOLDING SADNESS AND HOPE AT THE SAME TIME

We cannot deny the reality of our loss. We did not choose this path of suffering, but here it is. And because our world is saturated with duality, we often believe we will not be happy until the sadness stops. So we live in a suspended state of grief, waiting for relief from the pain. Conscious grieving offers an alternative. As we move into and learn from loss, conscious grieving invites us to allow both sadness and hope into our time of mourning, to open our hearts to both gratitude and loneliness in our grief. Conscious grieving calls us into non-dual awareness. Most of us are conditioned to think with a dualistic mind: "This is right or wrong." "I am happy or sad." "We are the good guys, and you are not." Duality can best be described as the "either/or" way of thinking. It is an unconscious world-view for most of us as we face the many choices of life. But life is more complex than this binary way of thinking. As Richard Rohr explains in *The Naked Now*,

> All-or-nothing thinking has caused me to make huge mis-takes and bad judgments, hurt people and myself, with-hold love and misinterpret situations. And this pattern of dualistic or polarity thinking is deeply entrenched in most Western people, despite its severe limitations. Binary thinking is not wrong or bad in itself—in fact, it is neces-sary in many if not most situations. But it is completely inadequate for the major questions and dilemmas of life.[10]

Binary thinking teaches a child when it is safe to cross the road. It establishes property lines and job descriptions. Binary think-ing provides structure when you have to make choices at the funeral home. It can create order. But, as Rohr states, it is inad-equate for life's dilemmas. While our grieving heart may seek comfort in this familiar mind-set, dualistic thinking restricts how we process loss: "Without my brother, I am not a sister." "Without my wife, I am not a husband." "Without him or her, I cannot be happy." Understandably, but regrettably, our dual experience of loss looks at who we are and sees who we are not.

Nondual or unitive consciousness arises out of our suf-fering as we struggle to accept the painful reality before us.

We are opened to a new way of being. Rohr explains that "when you are inside of . . . great suffering, you have a much stronger possibility of surrendering ego controls and opening up to the whole field of life. Frankly, because you do not have much choice now, you are being led."[11] Entering into nondual thinking offers a way to live in the dissonance of loss with more grace and less fear. Nondual consciousness eases our painful expectation of getting everything back to how it was and loosens our attachment to how things should be. Nonduality slowly opens our minds to embrace how life is, right now—even if that acceptance is just for a precious minute or two. It allows us to have a moment of peace amid our sadness. We find it okay to laugh at a silly joke, rather than shutting out those seconds of joy. In nondual thinking we see that the good things in life coexist with loss, that both are part of the fullness of being human. Unitive thinking helps us look through the pain to consider a life that includes love. We have room for both sweet memories of our loved one and the bitter reminder of the empty chair in front of us. As our capacity to hold these disparate emotions in our hearts grows, we increase our understanding of who we are and who we are becoming. We become larger in spirit, more hopeful in life, and happier in our hearts.

As the words often attributed to Washington Irving remind us, "There is a sacredness in tears. They are not a mark of weakness, but of power." The same can be said of our grief. Grief is not to be avoided but learned from. It is not a symptom of brokenness but a pathway toward transformation. Grief's sacred process helps us recover from loss with full and open hearts. Grief's tears return us to the truth of who we are . . . our most vulnerable, authentic self.

Promptings of Hope

Family therapist Pauline Boss, summarizing Auschwitz survivor Viktor Frankl's thinking, says that "without meaning there is no hope, and without hope there is no meaning." To increase your appreciation of nondual thinking, practice a new phrase in your thoughts and, perhaps, speech: *at the same time.* For example, when you look at the window expecting a sunny Saturday morning and instead see rain, your first thought might be, "Bummer, I wanted to work in the garden today!" Revise your perspective by adding the phrase *at the same time* and see what comes next: "I wanted to work in the garden today; at the same time, my flowers really need the rain." Or "I wanted to work in the garden today; at the same time, I love the smell of fresh rain." Practice this exercise in simpler situations pertaining to the weather, traffic, or food before moving on to relationships or beyond. This is a process of opening your mind to a "both/and" point of view.

"I really wanted to go out tonight; at the same time,
I could use the quiet."

"He acts like he knows everything; at the same time,
I could learn a lot from him."

"I'm afraid I won't know anyone there; at the same time,
it's good for me to meet new people."

"My heart breaks when I think of her; at the same time,
I am so grateful she was my mother."

CHAPTER 3

UNEXPECTED LANDMARKS AND LAND MINES

While we have been naming the resources you bring with you and looking over the terrain you might find in the Land of Loss, it is also important to identify some particular challenges ahead. You might confront patterns of behavior or points of view that limit or interfere with your healing. Guilt's sticky slime is a frequent presence in Alone, for example, often staying with us throughout the journey. Anger, sometimes hard to accept or admit, can also make an unmistakable appearance. Don't judge yourself if these reactions appear—or do not appear. Grief differs for each of us. Some of us seek to avoid the pain of loss altogether and rely upon life-limiting behaviors to manage our feelings. Look carefully as you survey the landscape before you. Get to know the parts of your story that trigger these unexpected reactions and offer yourself patience and compassion for being a human being. Your ownership of this trek is important, for it empowers confidence in yourself and in your potential for healing.

THE STICKY TRAP OF GUILT

Lana worried when her boyfriend, James, was diagnosed with cancer, but she also admitted feeling impatient and pressured. They had recently moved in together, with her daughter, to start a new life. Lana's mother was quite vocal in her disapproval of their unmarried arrangement. Lana tried to focus on her work, James, and her eleven-year-old daughter, but following the diagnosis she was overwhelmed with trying to balance everything. She felt guilty, thinking James's needs received short shrift. After James died, Lana tried to return to a normal life, but she couldn't rid herself of feelings of guilt. "What was wrong with me? He needed me and I wasn't there," she repeated throughout our sessions. Lana saw all her unloving choices and couldn't see anything else.

We expect to encounter sadness in the Land of Loss. Hopefully we've become patient with our disorientation in this new world, aware of the loneliness and vulnerability found there. But when we're faced with feelings of guilt, our reactions are often complicated. They may be linked to the deceased, the process of dying, or the reasons for the death, or they may surface as part of our childhood history. In Lana's case, her relationship with her mother was seeded with guilt, easily influencing her grief. Guilt may also be an unconscious cover-up of other feelings waiting beneath the surface. Guilt's presence, for example, can mask our fear as we face an unknown future. Guilt takes a toll on us in our grief. It can dominate our emotions and siphon our energy away from the healthy process of grieving.

The first step toward dealing with guilt is to become aware of the feelings and learn more about them. When we separate ourselves from unconscious patterns, we give them less power. All relationships carry mixtures of positive and negative feelings and memories, so a degree of guilt is normal in grief. The pain of loss can highlight past resentments toward a loved one, which can then create feelings of guilt: "How could I have been mad at him for that?" Our own imperfections, such as impatience or being judgmental, can become fodder for the growth of guilt's sticky slime. We turn on ourselves, remembering all the times we made bad choices or failed to love.

Tory Zellick, author and caregiving blogger, experienced guilt after her mother died. Tory had been her caregiver, seeing her mother through almost seven years of illness.

> This identity crisis was quickly followed by "what-ifs" and "should-haves": What if I had done a better job at fill-in-the-blank? What if we had chosen a different treatment option? I should have let her have that grilled cheese sandwich! I should have taken her to that movie! I should have been a better kid when I was five years old! The truth is, I did the best job I knew how, giving my mother 110 percent of my effort, time, and attention. I simply was torturing myself with 20/20 hindsight.[1]

Tory's story is an example of "illegitimate guilt," Therese Rando's term for when we hold ourselves to unreasonable—if not impossible—expectations. Illegitimate guilt, a normal response to loss, reflects the sudden lack of control that we confront in the face of death. In her grief Tory began to judge her care for her mother. Her guilt is termed "illegitimate" because it does not reference a true act of harm but more of a fear of not doing enough. In general, illegitimate guilt results from emotional responses to relationships that lack perfection. As human beings, though, we're not perfect. We make mistakes; we let people down. Our grief can lead us to look back with unreasonable expectations for ourselves. Sometimes we experience illegitimate guilt when we judge our feelings as wrong—feelings of abandonment following a husband's death turn into anger at him, and then we feel guilty for being angry. Another example is survivor guilt—the feeling that we should not be alive when a loved one isn't.

When we encounter illegitimate guilt in grief, talking with a trusted friend or counselor can create some distance from its sticky slime. When we put conscious effort into forgiving ourselves—preparing a list of the many ways we showed and shared love to balance the negative messages of guilt, for example—we are able to temper the unrealistic expectations we've been carrying.

Legitimate guilt is another story. According to Rando, this is guilt resulting from an act or failure to act that actually causes harm.

> This type of guilt occurs when there is a direct cause-and-effect relationship between what you did or failed to do and serious harm resulting to the deceased. In this situation, where your guilt is appropriate to the event, it must be acknowledged and plans must be made for restitution and expiation. This guilt can become destructive if you use it as self-punishment. When legitimate guilt warrants "punishment," you will need to do something constructive about it, such as doing something altruistic for others as a way of atoning.[2]

Darin Strauss's touching and award-winning memoir *Half a Life* tells the story of an eighteen-year-old's legitimate guilt following a car crash and the resulting death of a sixteen-year-old girl on a bicycle. He painfully describes the details of an innocent trip to play miniature golf resulting in twenty years of anguish, denial, and lack of self-forgiveness.

This moment has been, for all my life, a kind of shadowy giant. I'm able, tick by tick, to remember each second before it. Radio; friends; thoughts of mini-golf, another thought of maybe just going to the beach; the distance between car and bicycle closing; anything could still happen. But I am powerless to see what comes next; the moment raises a shoulder, lowers its head, and slumps away.[3]

As Darin's memoir reveals, the journey to move beyond legitimate guilt is profound and must be handled with care. His unfortunate experience with therapy stalled his recovery. He later gained some distance from his feelings through college, marriage, and child-rearing, but the guilt-turned-into-shame never left him. His writing became his path to atonement or expiation, as he shared his story on *This American Life* and later developed a memoir that acknowledged his humanness. Legitimate guilt requires this very deep look at ourselves and the circumstances. Most of us would benefit from professional help to sort through these feelings.

Promptings of Hope

Gary Zukav, founder of the Seat of the Soul Institute says on his website (seatofthesoul.com), "You cannot give the gifts that your soul wants you to give while you are feeling guilty." And that includes giving compassion to yourself on this journey of grief. If guilt is a part of your experience in the Land of Loss, use this exercise as an opportunity to lessen guilt's impact on your grief.

Try imagining your guilt as a sticky slime covering your body. See it? Notice its color; feel the sensation on your skin. It's everywhere, and it feels awful! Imagine that you have found a special cleaning liquid that was made to remove it. You've heard it works and you're willing to try. Take your time and imagine cleaning every inch of your body with this liquid grace—arms, face, legs, torso, even your hair. You may have to do this more than once and that's okay.

Each time you visualize this cleansing, imagine your guilt morphing into regret, which isn't as sticky. Keep using this hopeful imagery for the regrets that remain. Slowly, you may desire to release the guilt entirely. Over time, you may be willing to use forgiveness in your ritual of healing. Prayer and this creative cleansing offer further detachment from guilt's unnecessary presence. Focus on your desire to let go of guilt and to discover self-compassion.

ANGER: FROM LAND MINE TO LANDMARK

Every emotion has a story to tell, but we are often wrapped up in the experience of the emotion and unable to learn from it. When we become victims of these emotions, all we can do is hold on and try not to throw up. Much like guilt, anger is an emotion that is natural to grieving but also complicates it. Efforts to ignore or repress anger can steal our energy, leaving us exhausted, even debilitated. Author and grief counselor Stephen Levine explains, "It's our negative attachment to these emotions, our intense wish for them to be otherwise" that keeps us caught in their energy. "But," he goes on to say, "by moving toward these feelings we have always pulled away from and exploring them moment by moment, heartbeat to heartbeat, breath by breath, we come to see clearly their hidden nature."[4]

It is challenging for most of us to move toward our anger. We are conditioned to move away from it or hide it. For some of us, though, anger's explosive nature is hard to ignore. It might manifest as an outburst at the hospital staff or a waiter, at a red light, or even at ourselves. Unfortunately, few of us have a place where the real scream can be expressed, so we tend to repress anger, allowing it to do further damage to our broken hearts. For some, anger becomes a tension that requires constant vigilance to control, causing damage to our physical health. Research shows that repeated and repressed anger will dramatically and negatively influence heart health.

When Mark spoke about his son's death, his words were short, clipped. His mouth was tight, his voice controlled. It was as if he were holding back any secrets from spewing out of his mouth. When I asked about anger, Mark shrugged his shoulders and looked down at his hands. He seemed to be waiting as we sat together in the quiet. He shifted his body, unable to find a comfortable position, maybe unable to sit still with what was churning inside. These behaviors were in contrast to the man who walked into the office two weeks earlier, who told stories about his work and family, tears spilling over as he mentioned his son's name. But something had changed; something had triggered a rage that was palpable in the room. His son's death moved Mark to anger that day, and he didn't know what to do with the energy it created.

Mark tried to corral his anger but soon learned that was not going to help him get better. He, and all of us, need to find ways to express our feelings, even the explosive ones such as anger. The energy of anger can lead to violence. We painfully know this truth in our contemporary world. If your angry feelings lead to thoughts of hurting yourself or others, seek professional help immediately. For most of us, some anger is a normal response to the outrage of death. Conscious grievers are encouraged to see their anger, admit it to themselves and perhaps another, and give it a voice. As Levine reminds us, "When we investigate, we find beneath the grief of anger a reservoir of sadness. And beneath that sadness, an ocean of love beyond our wildest dreams."[5]

Anger can be a vent or a discharge of excess energy, but sometimes it serves as a cover-up or substitute for other feelings. Grief counselor Ashley Davis Bush explains:

> Anger is, in many ways, a "surface" emotion; it tends to mask a deeper feeling of pain and helplessness within. It's easier to be angry than sad. That's why for many, holding onto anger can last so long, because it's often easier than going to the next level deeper, to pain.[6]

If you have come upon anger on your journey through the Land of Loss, consider it as the headline of a story yet untold. Find ways to discharge its intensity and wait to learn what is underneath these powerful feelings. Physical exercise, writing, counseling, bodywork such as massage or Reiki all offer support. It is helpful to avoid judging anger as a bad emotion. Instead, look for what it can teach you about your relationship, your loved one, and yourself. Anger may even appear in your prayer, as you rage against your loss. Wrestling with God, however you define God, can stretch and deepen your faith experience.

Anger can also generate courage and cultivate inner strength in the face of the long path ahead. George Bonanno affirms that "anger in this case might help [the griever] develop a sense that she will be able to survive on her own."[7] Anger, at its core, served as a source of defense in our human evolution. For some of us today, anger can encourage the needed gumption to handle the maze of loss. Bonanno adds that anger may help us "deal with an ongoing battle with the medical bureaucracy, stand up to an insensitive friend, or hold our own in changing relations with friends and family."[8] Anger may play a helpful role in your grief, especially if it is seen through the lens of conscious grieving.

∽

Promptings of Hope

"And so I wait. I wait for time to heal the pain and raise me to my feet once again—so I can start a new path, my own path, the one that will make me whole again," writes Jessie Braun, a young adult dealing with loss, in *Chicken Soup for the Teenage Soul II*. She reminds us of the patience and bravery needed on this journey in the Land of Loss. Be brave as you look at the anger you might have and experiment with letting your anger speak. If you've felt some inklings of frustration or some rumblings of irritability, consider an experiment. Anger will adapt to any medium you choose for expression. This emotion fills our body with energy, seeking release. Privacy is a critical requirement for this type of grief-work. Your goal is to include as much of yourself—body, mind, and spirit—as you are able.

One way to release your anger is to write a letter to the illness that killed your beloved, to the fate that directed your destiny, or to God, who didn't listen to you. Share your outrage, frustrations, and sense of injustice. Use words that are strong and forceful to fully express your feelings. Use a thick, dark pen so the words stand out on the page, becoming a visible scream. If you are typing, hit the keys with force and intensity, as if you were hitting back at that which broke your heart.

Another way to release anger is to get physical. Hit the couch with a wiffle bat, stomp your feet, yell in the privacy of your car. Use the energy of your anger as a catalyst to dispense it. Let anger speak through the action of your body. Put your self-consciousness on the shelf for now. Your healing is more important than your judgment. Take a risk and be angry. With time, your experience of anger will change. It will dissipate, dissolve into tears, and perhaps lead you to silence.

CHOOSING ALTERNATE PATHWAYS

"Two roads diverged in a yellow wood." The imagery found in Robert Frost's poem "The Road Not Taken" is a reminder of the choices we constantly make while grieving. In Alone, much of our time and energy are taken up with survival. Our lives, the world around us, our hearts—everything has changed. It feels impossible to consider making a reasoned choice. Life demands our participation, though, and choices are everywhere. Just as we're faced with landmarks and land mines on the journey, we will also decide between life-giving and life-limiting behaviors, sometimes unconsciously. The results lead to very different landscapes.

Vincent's forty-year marriage filled his life, shaped his identity, and nurtured his loving heart. He relied on Antoinette in many ways and knew he was a better husband and father because of her. After Antoinette's death, Vincent felt lost. He stayed late at work and described his home as empty and lifeless. Vincent found himself avoiding his children and grandchildren because it hurt too much to be around them. But by avoiding the grandchildren to protect himself from the pain of loss, Vincent missed new joys and family moments as they grew up. As he hid from pain, he hid from life. The sad irony is that the memory of Antoinette, who was so full of life, became a trigger for life-limiting behaviors instead of an inspiration to live life.

Most of us deny our feelings at certain times as a defense mechanism. We've all been there. We experience a difficult coworker or a fender bender, but in the moment we don't fully take in how we feel. We tuck the facts away and get back to work or to the next thing. Later, when we are relaxed or alone, we remember what happened. With no more need to put that event on emotional hold, we let down our guard and feel the anger from the office encounter or fear from the accident.

After acknowledging and sitting with our feelings, we might make plans for the next step: speaking to the coworker or the boss, or canceling a trip while the car gets repaired. We create emotional boundaries as we make our way through loss as well. We seek distractions to provide a respite from the painful process of mourning. With our attention elsewhere, we are able to forget for a moment and regroup— take a so-called vacation from grief. A degree of respite makes sense; grieving is hard work. At the same time, these distractions can become habitual behaviors and strategies to avoid feeling our emotions. These avoidance patterns, or life-limiting behaviors, include taking on extra work, overeating, consuming alcohol, or watching countless hours of television. When we get pulled into the habit of avoiding our feelings, we keep our grief in a box. We end up compounding and complicating our grief and restricting our healing

If we can exchange life-limiting behaviors for life-giving ones—an important component of conscious grieving—our experience shifts. Life-giving behaviors nourish our grieving heart, opening it up to love. Each time we make a life-giving choice, we take another step in the direction of healthy and generative living. This is not always easy. Resistance and fear may reside within our feelings, subtly creating doubt around direct engagement with our grief. But when we take emotional risks and feel our feelings, we reconnect with our deepest places—where love and healing wait.

Fortunately, Vincent's love for his children and grandchildren helped him break out of the pattern of avoidance and gave him the courage to try something new. He started by gathering pictures, recipes, and the little sayings that Antoinette was known for. He put them on pages in a scrapbook and wrote a little commentary about each: where and when the picture was taken and what they were talking about at the time, a story about that particular meal or Antoinette's connection to that recipe, and his agreement or disagreement with Antoinette's famous saying. His goal was to capture these memories for his grandchildren's future.

This life-giving project supported Vincent on many levels. Most importantly, through this creative work he reconnected with the love of his life, Antoinette. He read her handwriting on the recipe cards, remembered her favorite sayings, and looked at her smiling face in the pictures. He found a way to tell her stories to the family, offering her the respect he felt she deserved. Since the scrapbook took a long time to fill, he worked on it periodically, giving purpose to his days and nights. She was once again a part of his life, and when he was done, she was a part of the family in a new and tangible way. Vincent's brave grief-work allowed him to remember that the great gift of love never truly dies.

Promptings of Hope

Human rights activist Nelson Mandela is often quoted as saying, "May your choices reflect your hopes, not your fears." Let this exhortation guide you as you mull over where life-giving and life-limiting choices appear in your life. Be gentle, not judgmental. All of us make the best decisions we can at the time. This is an opportunity to look at your patterns and learn from them. Grief's teachings are meant to return us to wholeness and to hope.

Write a list of your typical behaviors and activities during a week. For example: gardening, watching late-night television until 2 a.m., skipping breakfast, calling a friend, doing a crossword puzzle, and so on. After you have a list of at least twenty items, go back through and for each item ask yourself, "Is this activity adding life to my day (life-giving), or is it keeping me cut off from life (life-limiting)?" Label each item LG or LL as you think about this question. Be open to new thoughts that emerge. You may see that an activity that used to be life-giving (going to the cemetery every day) has changed. It has become life-limiting because you have less time for the gym. Reflect on what these categories mean to you, and on what life means to you right now.

PART 2

Passage

This region of the Land of Loss is known for its unexpected and constant movement. The traveler is pushed and pulled through and between the many complications of grief. For some, the journey is a roller-coaster experience that feels out of control and nauseating. Others find themselves lost in the Valley of Emptiness or searching the Forest of Anguish for relief. Inexperienced travelers brace themselves against the unpredictable shifts in terrain as they try to trust grief's guidance through the Land of Loss. The lessons learned here will support the rest of the journey, but they require hard work.

Our transition from Alone into Passage is movement away from shock and disbelief into an inescapable, demanding reality. Remember J. William Worden's four tasks of mourning? The first task was "to accept the reality of the loss." The second task, our motto in Passage, is "to process the pain of grief." There is no right or wrong way to feel, but feel we must. As Worden explains, "Not everyone experiences the same intensity of pain or feels it in the same way, but it is nearly impossible to lose someone to whom you have been deeply attached without experiencing some level of pain."[1] In Passage, we become aware of the many moving parts that shape our grief, from the outside world and from within ourselves. These influences, such as fears of the future, family expectations, or the community's response to our loss add to our unique experience. Passage demands adaptation, both in our identity and in our relationship with the world. This new terrain asks for a conscious emotional response to loss and ongoing self-compassion to continue moving through the process.

As we navigate the unpredictable turns in the Land of Loss, we learn more about our bodies as a resource for recovery. Our bodies hold a key to understanding the dramatic or subtle swings of grief, and neuroscience explains our built-in capacity for resilience. If we resist the fullness of this journey, we might never see what lies ahead. If we avoid experimenting with grief, we may depend on the patterns of the past that keep us going in circles. Trust what you have learned so far, take a deep breath, and step forward into Passage on your way toward healing.

CHAPTER 4

CHALLENGES
AND CHANGES
TO YOUR IDENTITY

Death challenges our understanding of who we are and how we are in the world. Confronted with the searing reality of loss, we are forced to examine our definition of ourselves. Are we still a brother if our only sibling has died, or a daughter if our only parent has passed away? Suddenly, and without our consent, our identity has changed. The transition into this new territory asks us to examine our development as individuals and the resulting effect of loss upon our sense of self. If we are to heal, we must trust in our capacity to heal and grow. There is no quick fix. But there is hope, for we humans have a remarkable gift for adaptation and recovery.

KNOWING OURSELVES

Jack's relationship with Marsha evolved over the sixteen years they shared an office. They became good friends, sharing family stories, laughter, and even occasional vacations. Marsha's house was Jack's second home, a safe place filled with the warmth of marriage and family. When Marsha died, Jack was confronted with her absence at work. Her empty desk and chair were inescapable. Visits with her family or plans for a trip to a faraway place became painful. Jack was devastated. He tried to make sense of his loss during our bereavement sessions and began talking about his own family. As Jack explained the dynamics in his family of origin, he began to see a connection to his grief. Marsha had filled his need for unconditional love, while his parents always seemed emotionally distant. She accepted and supported Jack as a gay man, unlike his parents, who seemed to merely tolerate this part of his identity. Jack chose to accept his parents and their limitations, but Marsha's death changed everything. Through his friendship with her, Jack had experienced the freedom to be himself. His grief became a process of knowing himself as Marsha knew him and reexamining the other relationships in his life.

From the minute we are born, our identity is shaped by the people in our lives. Our early, mostly dependent, relationships are especially influential, but throughout our lives relationships play a role in our evolution as individuals Thomas Attig describes these connections as "patterns of give-and-take," where we experience receiving and giving relational information with one another. Unspoken and spoken messages may communicate affirmation, togetherness, trust, reassurance, instruction, love, affection, intellectual stimulation, and so forth. They may also transmit ambivalence, threat, or lack of interest. Our identity evolves as these complex entanglements weave together, influencing us on many levels. As Robert A. Neimeyer explains,

> In a sense, we are all "pastiche personalities," reflecting bits and pieces of the many people whose characteristics and values we have unconsciously assimilated into our own sense of identity. This "inheritance" transcends

genetics, as we can be powerfully or subtly shaped not only by parents, but also by mentors, friends, siblings, or even children we have loved and lost. Nor are these life-imprints always positive: at times we can trace our self-criticism, distrust, fears, and emotional distance to once influential relationships that are now with us only internally.[1]

Understanding that our identity is shaped by a complex web of outside influences is in contrast to a culturally dominant way of thinking of ourselves as independent and impenetrable atoms in the universe. Many people believe identity is self-contained and Western individualistic values perpetuate that myth. Our personal understanding of identity either as self-contained and independent or as an intricate network of connections significantly influences our experience in the Land of Loss. As Attig tells us,

> If we accept the atomistic ways of thinking of ourselves we do not expect the shattering impacts of loss. Our relationships can and do mean a great deal to most of us, but few of us can appreciate how the connectedness that such relationships afford is integral to the unique persons that we are. Surprise at the nature, intensity, and pervasiveness of the effects of loss often unsettles us.[2]

When grief slows you down and places you in front of yourself, take some time with the idea that this particular relationship has been a part of who you are and how you grieve. Give yourself permission to sit before loss's mirror to explore the complexity of your connections. For example, while you experience sadness because she is gone, are you aware of threads of judgment that were part of the relationship? Or as you process the new world without him in it, are you encountering feelings of relief or, instead, a loss of confidence? With more knowledge about yourself, you travel the Land of Loss with more tools and, I'd suggest, more hope. No longer a victim to the pain of loss, you bring the most reliable resource you have—yourself.

Promptings of Hope

Reinhold Niebuhr's Serenity Prayer offers a voice of sanity and hope as you embrace the unique person you are: "God, grant me the serenity to accept the things I cannot change, the courage to change the things I can, and the wisdom to know the difference."

Empty a shelf, buy a notebook, or find a special bowl. Use one of these containers to establish a sacred space for yourself. Let it hold sources of support that you have (or would like to have) as you go forward. Write down insights or collect small, symbolic objects to remind yourself of what or who you can count on in this time of confusion. Over time, add each item to your sacred space as a reminder and a promise of hope. A small rock may speak of the hiking trail that opens your heart. The word *believe* might bring you back to Christmas memories of joy. The postcard from Barcelona, your granddaughter's ribbon, that quote from the Bible—gather them up and create a comforting presence designed just for you. These reminders will offer a healing salve on your wound of loss as you travel through your feelings. Possible themes to think about . . .

- People I can count on
- Places that bring calm to my heart
- Music that comforts me
- Beliefs that give me strength

- Objects I like to hold or look at
- Poems, quotes, and words of encouragement that lift me up or speak my truth
- Writers, artists, movie and book characters, saints, and other people in the world who face challenges bravely; folks who are role models for grieving

LOSING OURSELVES

The complex connections or entanglements of our relationships not only influence our early formation, they also illustrate the powerful impact of loss on our evolving self. After a death, everything in us longs to push a reset button, to return to the life that was so we can feel "normal" again. Barbara Lazear Ascher tells us, "You pine for home until you realize that what you long for is you as you once were—life as it once was."[3] Ascher's poignant truth, written following the death of her brother, reveals the feeling of disorientation that often accompanies the challenges of grief. We become aware of losing *ourselves* in addition to our loved one. This may create other confusing feelings—especially, if we judge such awareness as self-centered. "Shouldn't I focus all my attention on my loved one? That's who I'm grieving, right?" To clarify, we are *mourning* our loved one through an expression of sorrow. Our *grief*, however, is our own and it responds to our unique loss.

For a minute, visualize yourself with multiple antennae—hundreds of waving, alive receptors of energy. Imagine that each one is tuned in, uniquely, to each of the people you know, activating a specific antenna in you and a specific antenna in the other person. Shared jokes, moments of quiet, passion, insights discovered together, tension, buttons that get pushed and demand growth—all come alive when our antennae are in sync with another. When someone dies, there is no one else tuned into the frequency of that specific antenna. No one. We feel truly cut off from our unique experience with that one specific person.

Our reactions to this loss of connectedness vary. Some of us try to fill the void, staying busy, adding new activities, jumping into new relationships. This may bring some distraction, even comfort, but these outcomes are often unsatisfying. Something is still missing. Others of us just stop sending energy to that particular antenna; it hurts too much without him or her. So instead of giggling at old movies as you always did with Uncle Fred, you stop watching them to avoid feeling his absence. This offers a defense against the pain you feel after death. Unfortunately, when you shut down painful emotions, positive and life-giving emotions are dragged into the void as well. Ignoring or turning away from that stranded antenna denies the truth of who you are and limits your connection to yourself.

Dr. Abraham Twerski, a rabbi and psychiatrist, reminds us that "in his classic paper *Mourning and Melancholia*, Sigmund Freud describes a close interpersonal relationship as having 'feelers' extending from one person to another. When the person toward whom these feelers are directed dies, the feelers are left dangling in midair."[4] The lonely experience of "losing ourselves" in Passage echoes our experience in Alone, as our antennae or feelers search and search and come up empty. Every new situation, person, or event demands the same internal response: "Yes, she is gone." "Yes, he died." Our partially healed wound goes back to its raw state. We are reminded over and over that life has changed. The unspoken question waits for an answer, "How will all this change taking place *around me*, change who I *am*?"

While it is normal to move back and forth between the territories in the Land of Loss, it is unsettling. Especially when your sense of self is changing. Your vulnerability increases as the feeling of disconnection becomes part of everyday life. Alan Wolfelt confirms,

> You may feel child-like as you struggle with your changing identity. You may feel a temporarily heightened dependence on others as well as feelings of helplessness, frustration, inadequacy, and fear. These feelings can be overwhelming and scary, but they are actually a natural response to this important need of mourning.[5]

It is natural to fear this disorientation. We've lost our loved one, and now our sense of self; life is now defined by the desolation of grief. We may see hope alive in someone else's life, but not in our own. There is no quick fix for this experience. We might have found a way to cope with past losses, but this particular one is different. This loss changed us in a new way, and stubborn endurance is not working. In this ungrounded, disconnected place, we must turn to self-compassion to bring added healing to our broken heart. We must return to love.

We know love. It is our human nature to care for each other. If another is hurt or upset, we usually respond with concern and support. We experience compassion as we suffer with another human being's struggle. This is so natural, yet it's surprising how unnatural it feels to extend that same compassion, care, and concern to ourselves. Self-compassion must be an intentional act, otherwise we neglect our hurting hearts. We forget, as psychotherapist Francis Weller reminds us, that "we, too, are part of this breathing, pulsing world . . . that, by the mere fact of being here, we qualify for the soothing waters of compassion."[6] In this upended place of change, we thirst for such waters. Our hearts cry out and ask that we take ourselves by the hand toward the water's edge, leading ourselves into its cooling comfort and waiting patiently together.

In describing the gift of self-compassion, Weller reminds us to give up the "agenda of self-improvement." Too often, he explains, we believe "that our weakness or inadequacy, our neediness or our failures are the reasons for our suffering, and *if only* we could be free of them, we would enter into a state of perfection, all would be well."[7] This traditional attitude will not support us in the lonely, disconnected spaces of Passage or anywhere in the Land of Loss. Grief is not a process of self-improvement but a process of healing. Soothe your stranded, confused self in the waters of self-compassion. Give yourself the regard and tenderness you would offer to any other living being.

Promptings of Hope

Carl Jung tells us, "Your vision will be clear only when you look into your heart. Who looks outside dreams. Who looks inside awakens." As painful as it is, grief provides us with the opportunity to turn inward to examine who we are and who we want to become.

In an exercise called "Defining and Envisioning Self," grief counselor Vicki Panagotacos suggests asking yourself four questions:

1. What do you want to include in your life?

2. What don't you want to include in your life?

3. What do you have in your life that you want to eliminate?

4. What do you have in your life that you want to keep?[8]

Spend some time with these questions in two or three different sessions. Write down your answers each time. You may notice that your answers change over time. End each session with relaxed breathing and quiet reflection time.

In the closing session, look at the final list for "What do you want to include in your life?" Take each answer (keep my apartment, volunteer at the shelter, learn how to meditate, take dance lessons) and write down steps that will bring your desire into being. Tuck these ideas away and trust that the flow of your grief will direct your action when the time is right. For now, savor your capacity to listen to your own wisdom, your own truth.

TRUSTING OURSELVES

We understand the feeling of the lost connection, whatever language we use to describe it—relationship, the bond, the antennae, or the bits and pieces we've received and given one another. One part of our grief-work is to recognize and grieve the absence of this connection. Another part is to reweave the strands of connectedness, to regain wholeness as we relearn ourselves. Grief provides both the time and space and the guidance for this process. When we step into our grief as a participant, we see the road ahead more clearly. If we respect, learn from, and take care of our hurting heart, we become part of the healing. We're not talking about speeding up the journey, but trusting it and ourselves.

Mandy's life with Stan was everything she had hoped for. They had been friends first, then as the years passed, their relationship became romantic. When they moved in together, their families were happy for them, including Stan's ex-wife and his sisters. When Stan died, Mandy felt cheated, since their life together had been so brief. She sought help with her grief and found comfort in knowing much of what she was experiencing was normal. As Mandy trusted the process, she began to listen to her sadness, anger, guilt, and loneliness. She experimented with journal writing to express her feelings and decided to follow her instincts to memorialize Stan. Mandy reached out to Stan's sisters and planned a get-together to remember him during the holiday season. She later invited family members to select some of his memorabilia to share his legacy. The following spring, she helped the family plan and participate in a town ceremony that honored his military accomplishments. In each situation, Mandy trusted her needs as valid and supported others' needs along the way. Her actions strengthened her confidence in herself and her connection with Stan.

This transition into trust does not always happen easily. Our reliance on anything and everything is eroded by the confusion of loss. Thomas Attig explains, "When we are bereaved we experience divisions within ourselves as the webs of our lives are torn asunder. . . . We experience ourselves as suspended between a reality where we were at home and knew how to be ourselves and a reality transformed by loss where we have yet to find our way."[9]

But self-trust can be cultivated. It provides a way to ground yourself while traveling through the Land of Loss. As a doorway into your values, faith, feelings, confidence, and integrity, self-trust leads you into your deepest places. It means you can count on yourself, that you will take care of yourself as best you can. Author and therapist Cynthia Lynn Wall tells us, "To say 'I trust myself' means you take care of your own needs and safety and are a loving force in your life."[10] Self-trust nurtures the unattached antennae as you find your way and lets you admit, "This is who I am," even when you feel out of place or misunderstood. As Wall describes, "Self-trust supports your ability to explore new choices and tackle big challenges. It means opening to a bigger definition of who you really are and what you are capable of doing."[11]

While trust may not come easily in this vulnerable place of grief, Wall offers tips we can use to help our inner trust grow:

Explained through the lens of loss, these suggestions provide another set of tools for our journey. With practice, they will strengthen our sense of self as we are reacquainted with our evolving identity.

KEEP PROMISES TO YOURSELF. Every time we keep a commitment we have made to ourselves, we increase trust. When faced with loss, it's important to keep these promises simple and small: "I will walk outside three times a week." "I will take a nap when I am tired." "I will call my sister tomorrow." The follow-throughs accumulate, each building on the other, and remind you that you are worth this commitment.

AVOID PEOPLE WHO UNDERMINE YOUR SELF-TRUST. While the goal here is not to end relationships, it is helpful to notice who is supportive and who is not. When we are grieving we sometimes must protect ourselves from well-meaning family and friends. They may offer suggestions and opinions that are confusing, even judgmental. They may be unaware that their contributions are based on their own feelings about loss and grief, and may not necessarily help yours. The development of self-trust may require establishing clear emotional boundaries.

SPEAK KINDLY TO YOURSELF. Most of us say things to ourselves that we would never say to another person. We become impatient, for example, and hear an inner critic say, "You aren't doing this right! When are you going to learn?" Listening to such inner voices does not help and can be destructive, particularly to a broken heart. To build self-trust, make an effort to speak to yourself with love, kindness, and respect. Patiently remind yourself that you are doing the best you can with the demands of your grief.

Promptings of Hope

"I have been trying to make the best of grief and am just beginning to learn to allow it to make the best out of me," writes Barbara Lazear Ascher in *Landscape without Gravity*. Conscious grieving calls for this cooperative attitude toward the lessons of loss. As you cultivate self-trust, be patient. Each step along the way is an opportunity to affirm and reaffirm yourself. Use this exercise to explore the connection between who you are and the things you like and trust about yourself.

Write a list of ten things you like about yourself, such as:

- I'm reliable.
- I'm good at wrapping presents.
- I volunteer at the soup kitchen.

Then, for each item, create a connection with trust or the quality of being trustworthy. For example:

- I'm reliable. People can rely on me; I am trustworthy.
- I'm good at wrapping presents. My wrapping brings beauty to the occasion. I can trust in my ability to make packages pretty.
- I volunteer at the soup kitchen, I trust my capacity to care for others.

Don't let this simple exercise fool you. Your efforts to align yourself with trust will increase your confidence in yourself and in your capacity to trust.

OUR GUIDES
AND OUR GATEKEEPERS

"Grief is like a long valley, a winding valley where any bend may reveal a totally new landscape. . . . Not every bend does. Sometimes the surprise is the opposite one; you are presented with exactly the same sort of country you thought you had left behind miles ago."[1] C. S. Lewis reminds us that there is always a degree of unpredictability in our travels through the Land of Loss. The unexpected is part of the challenge as we look around corners, waiting for what is going to jump out. At the same time, there are factors that can help us understand the landscape. Our unique past, for example, influences how we grieve; so do the circumstances of our loved one's death. Future concerns and fears shape today's grief as well. The terrain also includes the community around us. Their support—or lack of it—influences our private experience of grief.

The collection of characteristics that pertain to you, your life, and your loved one forge your individual journey. When you name the various elements that come together, you establish a map of the possible turns or gates up ahead. The combinations that create an individual's journey appear limitless and can seem overwhelming. As you read through the following descriptions of past, present, and future influences on grief, pause and look for yourself in some of these categories. Remember, most of these influences are *givens* in the world of you and me; they are unchangeable. But our awareness of these circumstances can help us take care of ourselves within the ups and downs of Passage. Getting to know your unique story in this strange new land is key to conscious grieving.

THE PAST: WHO WE BRING TO THE LOSS

Our childhood and any of our years of life before a death set the stage for how we respond to that particular loss. We cannot do anything about these precedent factors, but they help us see our grief within the context of our lives. As we accept our family background, our personality, or the ups and downs of our relationship with our loved one, for example, we move closer to our own authenticity. Once there, in a place of honesty and vulnerability, we more easily accept our humanness and our lack of control. We more easily accept ourselves and our grief.

GENDER

Men and women both experience loss with a wide range of emotions. Sex-role conditioning, however, can result in different expectations for expression of those feelings. It is typically easier for women to yield to the process of grief because men are often expected to manage and control their feelings. Women tend to be more overtly emotional and rely upon social support. Men, who tend to be more practical, more commonly turn to physical activities and problem-solving to cope with their loss.

PERSONALITY

As in life, our basic nature affects how we respond to grief. Extroverted, introverted, shy, sunny, dramatic, methodical—each of us understands and experiences loss uniquely. Acceptance and appreciation of our individuality will enable a healthy grieving process.

COPING STYLES

We respond to loss the same way we respond to other challenges in life. Some people try to avoid them; others meet them head-on. Some ask for help, and others stubbornly refuse it. Our maturity and the methods we use to manage or survive life circumstances shape our interaction with the demands of grieving as well.

EXPRESSION OF GRIEF AS TAUGHT BY FAMILY, CULTURE, ETHNICITY, AND RELIGION

The formational elements from our family of origin influence our response to loss. This template often guides our approach as adults. Cultural attitudes are also planted deep within us, whether we are aware of them or not. Religious beliefs and traditions surrounding death and grief add to the encompassing message that is passed on from one generation to the next. While these patterns are ingrained, as adults we can review them and explore their usefulness for this particular loss.

FORMATION THROUGH CHILDHOOD ATTACHMENT

Our relationship with our primary caregiver is known as an attachment. Researchers identify the different kinds of attachment as secure, insecure, or uncertain. Each of these influences our process of grieving in a different way. Secure, reliable attachments in childhood offer the strongest base for our adult response to loss. Conversely, insecure attachments add to the distress that loss creates. Uncertain or unpredictable attachments establish an unreliable base for a child, which leads to varying difficulties in grief for the adult. Similar to our familial and cultural patterns, attachment formation has a strong, persistent impact on our adult response to loss. Awareness, however, can lead to inner work and growth to support further healing.

HISTORY OF DEPRESSION OR ADDICTIVE BEHAVIORS

Our mental health impacts all aspects of life—relationships, professional success, and any personal experiences, such as loss. Depression, for example, complicates grief, and their similarity at the outset can be confusing. Clinical depression, unlike grief, is a long-lasting medical condition that requires professional support and an understanding of its influence on the grieving process. Addictive behaviors can delay healthy grieving as they cripple our emotional life and health. Drugs, alcohol, food, overwork, and other addictive behaviors hamper the normal process of grief that is asking us to feel our feelings, not avoid them.

PAST EXPERIENCES OF LOSS

Subtle, intense, few, or frequent—your past losses are part of you. Those that were unprocessed will become part of the mix, their incomplete healing influencing future experiences of loss. Those losses that led to a healing experience serve as a template and source of comfort for each new and different loss.

THE NATURE OF THE RELATIONSHIP ITSELF

Your relationship with your loved one may have been loving, with well-established bonds of trust. It may have been tense and challenging, or it could have included unfinished business or a history of estrangement. The role your loved one played in the family or social system is part of the relationship as well. These variations in relationship weave into the experience of loss and the resulting grief. An honest look at the nature of your relationship opens the gate for real feelings and real healing.

THE PRESENT: THE LOSS ITSELF

The trauma of this one loss, at this particular time of your life, places its own set of demands on your energy and emotions. To appreciate the depth and breadth of these influences on your grief, think of watching a friend go through what you just experienced. How did shock register on his face? How is she handling being alone? With this perspective, perhaps you can care for yourself with greater compassion and patience. You are probably overwhelmed in an effort to comprehend and survive the trauma of your loved one's death. All of the following factors can play a part in your grief experience.

SUDDEN DEATH OR PROLONGED ILLNESS AND DEATH

The shock of a sudden death reverberates through our bodies. What we know as real has changed without warning, sometimes so quickly that emotions virtually spin. Much of our energy is used to try to catch up to the new reality, as the anguish of loss sets in. There is no preparation, only bewildered reaction.

If you've traveled with a loved one's painful or debilitating illness, you may end up grieving before death actually happens. Anticipatory grief is a normal response during a lingering illness. Numbness, confusion, and anger can appear out of order, before your loved one has died, complicating your grief. In some cases, when death finally happens, you might feel relief because the suffering is over, and then quickly feel guilty for feeling that moment of respite. Sometimes you grieve the loss of the intimate caregiving experience, in addition to the loss of your loved one. Whatever the circumstances, your emotions, body, and spirit all react in their own way and in their own time.

THE AGE OF THE DECEDENT

The death of a young person turns the natural order on its head. The anguish of this loss often requires specialized support since the complications are far-reaching. The loss of a peer can set off fears of our own mortality, and the loss of an elder can upend the family unit. Our feelings about our loved one's time of life deserve acknowledgment and expression.

TRAUMATIC CIRCUMSTANCES

Violent deaths such as murder or suicide create unique and difficult grief. Layers of shock and disbelief are compounded by horror, anger, or guilt. If you've lost a loved one in military action, you may be comforted by pride in their service, but at the same time the trauma of a violent death might haunt your grief. Some people are confronted with more than one loss in a relatively short time period; the grief of multiple losses becomes a lifestyle, a type of quicksand that can make our previous selves feel unrecoverable. Traumatic circumstances exacerbate our grief and usually require grief support.

THE COMMUNITY'S ACCEPTANCE OF DEATH

We do not grieve alone. We are part of families, communities, churches, and more. Our grief experience is usually aided by the support of these groups. There are circumstances, however, where our community can hinder our healing, such as when they minimize the loss or disenfranchise our grief. We'll discuss more about this later.

LONG-DISTANCE DEATH

Deaths that occur far away create a special challenge for most of us. We can almost pretend it isn't true, which coincides with our heart's desire, because our loved one isn't part of our daily life. Friends and neighbors who do not know our loved one have less awareness of our loss. When services are held far away, we have less public support in our own community. Through circumstances imposed by geography, our loss's significance is somehow lessened.

THE FUTURE: CONCERNS UP AHEAD

Every death has subsequent factors that influence grief. These add complications after the funeral is over and after the sympathy cards stop coming. In some cases, these ongoing ripple effects prevent the grief itself from settling in or settling down. You may attempt to return to a normal world and find that normal has changed. Awareness of these influences reminds us to catch our breath, add self-care, or get extra support as the process continues.

LEGAL OR CRIMINAL ISSUES

If our loss becomes enmeshed in the legal system, we might find ourselves waiting and wondering. The timing of our personal grief is not aligned with police investigations, prosecutions, and courtrooms. Your hope that justice will heal the pain of loss can be misleading. Consequently, your grief process can be stalled by forces far beyond your control and your loved one's memory gets tangled up in all of it.

PRESSURE FROM FAMILY OR FRIENDS

Many well-intentioned friends, neighbors, and family members still believe that grief should be completed within a certain time frame. "Have you thought about taking off your ring?" said at the sixth-month anniversary of a husband's death. "You can always have another one," offered to a young woman three months after she buried her newborn baby. "Are you thinking about dating?" asked of a man who has not yet cleaned out his wife's clothes. These remarks add pressure and self-doubt when you are trying to remember your loved one, honor his or her memory, and heal from the pain of the loss. These moments call for confidence in the process and in yourself. Your grief is your own to understand and navigate.

THE AGE AND HEALTH OF THE BEREAVED

Your well-being is significant in the grief process. The first cold or flu without your loved one can trigger a loss experience in and of itself. Any health fears, aging issues, or physical fragility that you have influences your grief, as you are blatantly reminded of your own vulnerability. Again, patience and self-compassion are the best forms of self-care.

WORK LIFE AND FINANCIAL SECURITY

Employment or meaningful activity might provide a helpful alternative to the emptiness of grief. On the other hand, work can be overwhelming and demand too much from your broken heart. People with concerns about finances often experience extra instability during the challenging emotional process of grief. It is reasonable to feel unsettled in response to uncertain work or financial situations in your life.

SECONDARY LOSSES

The death of our loved one is known as the primary loss. The secondary losses unfold as we walk through the Land of Loss. On one level, secondary losses include the loss of her income or contact with his friends. But we may fear the loss of his legacy when he is gone or lose our confidence without her support. We could lose our purpose in life or our feelings of joy. A wife, grieving the death of her husband, can experience the secondary losses of losing her accountant, lover, gardener, problem solver, humorist, and best friend, all compounding her grief. As you uncover the many ways you are connected to

your loved one, pay attention and consider the extra grieving
that each layer of loss might require.

Promptings of Hope

A wise saying often attributed to Jesuit philosopher Teilhard
de Chardin reminds us that "We are not human beings having
a spiritual experience, we are spiritual beings having a human
experience." Each of the elements of your personal story are part
of your precious human experience. Take some time to review
them and note one or two factors from your past, present, and
future that stand out. You might choose "unfinished business"
since that is a new idea for you or "your role as caregiver" because
you just want to think about that a little more.

Write each topic on a small piece of paper, place the pieces of
paper next to a lit candle, and give yourself ten to twenty minutes
of quiet reflection for each one. Let your thoughts, feelings, and
memories surrounding your story surface and subside as they
wish. Give yourself permission to see the caregiver's influence,
for example, on your grief without judgment. Are you aware of
the feelings that role created in you? Or if unfinished business
is your focus, gently ask yourself what was left undone in the
relationship. No judgment, no plan, but a patient, loving look
at your story. You are just checking out the underbrush in the
landscape, getting to know it a little better. When you are done,
blow out the candle and find a spot to save the pieces of paper.
Such sacred reflection time warrants your respect and you may
want to return to your reflections at another time.

THE COMMUNITY'S RESPONSE

Have you ever driven by a display of flowers and crosses on
the side of a road? Or waited in your car as a line of drivers

follows a hearse and limousine through the stoplights in your town? Have you participated in a moment of silence at a sports event to recognize someone's passing? These rituals, and many more, have been created to cope with the inescapable truth of loss. At the same time, each speak to our interconnectedness. We think of the one who has left and the many who grieve him or her. In these instances—seeing a spontaneous floral display, observing a funeral cortege, participating in a moment of silence—we silently agree that this death deserves our acknowledgment; this life, our respect. Through these acts of mourning, we join with the experience of loss and grief and our membership in the human family.

In most cases, we live in community and we die in community. Historically, our responsibility to the deceased, includes "three post-death tasks: (a) to dispose of bodies appropriately, (b) to make real the implications of death, and (c) to work toward social reintegration and healthful ongoing living," according to social psychologist Charles A. Corr.[2] Both body preparation and our rituals for mourning have evolved over time and across cultures. While those of us who are integrated into a faith community follow a prescribed pattern, there are those who resist the expectation of shared ritual. As we will see, the community's response, or lack of it, to our loss will impact our grief.

Following a death, our participation in formal rituals often happens on autopilot. Someone leads us through the choices at the funeral home, for example, while our heart and mind are in a fog of confusion. We fall back on tradition to establish order in the chaos and time to honor our loved one. When the community gathers, they affirm the importance of our loss and provide emotional support for our grief. As anthropologist Margaret Mead writes, "I know of no people for whom the fact of death is not critical, and who have no ritual by which to deal with it."[3]

In our contemporary age, public rituals often include digital expression, which deserves a mention. Some find the cyber-connections helpful; others seek the human touch. As professor of family studies Kathleen R. Gilbert and marriage and family therapist Gloria D. Horsley point out:

> The Internet has no cultural boundaries or rules that govern how the deceased are memorialized. Freedom of expression through poetry, art, music, and writing is unrestricted. . . . Also, expressive sites such as the creation of a web memorial, unlike most post-death rituals, can be created at one's own pace.[4]

Death announcements and condolences are commonly expressed through social media, as the digital world has become mainstream. While there are opportunity and freedom in this form of expression, there is also reason to be cautious. In an essay written following the death of her thirty-six-year-old husband, Taya Dunn challenges the immediacy of technology in the context of grief and advises that we "give the immediate family or circle a little time to handle the immediate and time-sensitive 'business' related to death. In the minutes and early hours after someone passes away, social media is most likely the last thing on their minds."[5]

Community rituals of all varieties have an important place in our grief. They communicate to those suffering from the loss, "Your grief is understandable" and "Your loss is recognized." We can then relax in these public spaces because our grief is accepted and supported. Public acknowledgment enfranchises our grief—our right to have and to express our feelings is recognized. When a bereaved wife is escorted to the front of the church, for example, the community is surrounding her with prayer and with the shared expression of their own grief. She can feel their support somewhere in the midst of her pain, giving her the courage to keep going. When a father is asked to attend a peer-led memorial service to honor his son, he returns to his son's high school with a broken heart. At the same time, when students and staff speak of his son with affection, his loss is acknowledged and his heart heals just a little.

Jewish tradition provides a profound example of the gift of enfranchisement. The moment the grave is closed, undivided attention is given to the mourner. In traditional Judaism, the mourners—family members, for example—"sit shiva," which is seven days of gathering and prayer at the mourners' home. The mourners do not need to greet or welcome others, but simply receive their support without the social expectation of saying thank you. The community provides meals and may share memories of the deceased to offer comfort, but it is done as a mitzvah—a gift given freely. As the loving energy and prayers of the community focus on the mourners, they receive both deep and practical support. They are enfranchised in the best sense of the word.

When public rituals enfranchise our grief, they offer emotional, psychological, and spiritual freedom as we travel through the Land of Loss. The community's support through ritual and beyond sustains the hard work of grief through the connection of relationship. We are comforted by the reminder that we are not separate from each other, like individual trees in a forest or islands in the sea. Instead, we experience a coming together, a communion of hearts, knowing that, as philosopher William James puts it, "the trees also commingle their roots in the darkness underground, and the islands also hang together through the ocean's bottom."[6] The community, at its best, gathers up our private fears in its loving arms and becomes a reliable part of our healing.

Promptings of Hope

In Matthew 5:4, we read, "Blessed are those who mourn, for they will be comforted." This beatitude in Christian scripture offers a blessing of solace to those who grieve. It is a promise that comfort will be given, both by God and by God's people. As you reflect on the public support you received after your loved one died, identify the people who were particularly supportive and the activities that were helpful. Pull out the program from the funeral or the obituary from the newspaper. If there are no physical items like these, write a short list of your memories of communal activities: coffee time with your best friend, cleaning off the headstone with your family, the flowers distributed at the graveside. Use imaginative thinking to let these images surround you, creating a circle of support as you stand inside your grief. Let the affection, respect, and love of others reach out to you from that circle and share your loss, just a little, but just enough.

SOCIAL DENIAL OF GRIEF

Kenneth Doka, a leading expert in grief and grief counseling, introduced the term "disenfranchised" to describe grief that is not recognized or honored by others. Simply put, disenfranchised grief means that "survivors are not accorded the right to grieve."[7] If your grief is minimized or misunderstood, you may resonate with the idea of disenfranchised grief. You may find relief as this label helps untangle a feeling you can't quite name. Grief that is not acknowledged or socially supported can become complicated and even delayed. Once identified, though, disenfranchisement becomes a pathway into a fuller, more conscious grief, and allows more movement in the Land of Loss.

Disenfranchisement is not necessarily an intentional act to limit another's grief, but the results are the same whether it is intentional or not. For example, an elderly widow without a religious tradition decides to forgo any funeral services for her husband. As a result, her adult children and their families do not experience the network of support typically found through a traditional funeral, burial, and reception. While the wife's needs to "move on" are her own, her actions create a disenfranchised grief experience for the family. As Charles A. Corr writes,

> Bereavement rituals are intended precisely to seek or provide social recognition, legitimation, and support in times of loss and grief. Specific rituals may fall out of favor and no longer serve these purposes for the society as a whole or for some of its members. But to assume that such rituals can simply be abandoned without replacement, that people only mourn in private or exclusively personal ways, or that society can satisfactorily conduct its affairs and serve its members without any ritual whatsoever in times of death is to misconceive the needs of human beings and expose the dangers involved in disenfranchised grieving.[8]

In *Disenfranchised Grief: New Directions, Challenges, and Strategies for Practice*, Kenneth Doka suggests five categories of loss that can lead to the social denial of grief. As you read these explanations and examples, keep in mind that you alone know if your grief has been acknowledged and supported. If it has not, stay open to the idea that within the absence of social support lies the opportunity for your own creative grieving practices. As in the other regions of the Land of Loss, your active participation with your grief will support your healing.

THE RELATIONSHIP IS NOT RECOGNIZED

Relationships that are outside the family structure may be overlooked or sometimes unknown. The experience of loss corresponds to the closeness of the relationship, not just the biological or kin-based connection. The partner of a closeted gay person may fail to receive needed acknowledgment and support if the relationship is not recognized at the time of death. The death of a neighbor, tennis partner, or professional colleague may not qualify for bereavement time off, but the loss may still be significant.

If your relationship is not recognized by the greater community, your grief might be inviting you to honor its significance in your life. You may choose to honor him privately through a donation or recognize her contributions with a public event—a tennis match or a dinner party. Your grief might be urging you to value and express the gift of this relationship, leading you past the missing acknowledgment toward your own truth.

THE LOSS IS NOT RECOGNIZED

Social definitions of loss can influence our personal experience of grief. Loss of pets, jobs, health, or fertility, for example, are often disregarded losses, and the subsequent grief is minimized. People mistakenly dismiss a miscarriage as an insignificant loss, believing an unborn child does not yet exist. Therese Rando states,

> In this case . . . they fail to realize the attachment that existed from the time of awareness of pregnancy. There have been fantasies, needs, hopes, dreams, and expectations placed upon this child-to-be, all of which are profound losses in addition to the actual physical death of the baby.[9]

When loss is not seen as a loss by others, the disconnect causes us to doubt our own feelings. It is easy in these situations to be critical and judgmental of ourselves. This insidious form of disenfranchisement undermines our loss and our grief and calls for a response if we are to move toward healing. With courage in our hearts, we might look for support from those with similar experiences. We might use creative personal ritual to honor the significance of our loss.

THE GRIEVER'S NEEDS ARE EXCLUDED

Those who are very young or in the throes of dementia are often overlooked at the time of death. There is a mistaken belief that they have little comprehension of the loss. People with mental illness or disabilities may also be disenfranchised under the same misunderstanding, denying their emotional and social needs.

Avoiding this form of disenfranchisement requires the extra care of another to support their grieving. It calls upon the best in us to be attentive to those with special needs, so they may be heard and affirmed. A simple acknowledgment of absence may be all that is needed, but such a gesture affirms the humanity of the griever and the life of the deceased. When we respond to disenfranchisement in this way, we enter the mystery of love.

THE CIRCUMSTANCES OF THE DEATH

The nature of the death can influence social support. A son's suicide, for example, may create a sense of stigma for the parents. They could feel uncomfortable talking about his death and, subsequently, his life. Neighbors want to help but find themselves withdrawing instead. Other circumstances, such as murder, the death of an active alcoholic, or an AIDS-related loss can inhibit much-needed support, as people sometimes avoid these complicated situations.

Special circumstances are often best supported by groups with like losses. The general population may not be able to offer the acknowledgment that is needed and deserved. With help, though, those grieving a complicated death find a safe place to grieve and the courage to acknowledge their loss. Their healing helps others in their life deepen their awareness and compassion for loss through difficult circumstances, which in turn can reverse some of the disenfranchisement. This is not easy and not always accomplished, but it is a path of hope.

The Way Someone Grieves

We may discount someone's loss if their emotional expression, or lack of it, does not fit with our expectations of how someone should grieve. Someone who has very private grief, who doesn't share their emotions easily, may be judged as grieving inadequately. Another who is highly emotional can be seen as "too dramatic" or trying to get attention. Acknowledgment and support are withheld after such an evaluation of the individual's style of grief.

Our grief is our own. It is shaped by a myriad of influences. If our grief is disenfranchised because it makes someone else uncomfortable, we can't fix that. We are entitled to our feelings and personal style, to our unique journey through the Land of Loss. It is not unusual for relationships to change after loss. At the same time, if we find our important relationships are being affected by our grief, we may want to learn from these situations. Counseling, for example, could help sort out our feelings. Grief often calls us toward the both/and of life and deserves our attention.

Creative, conscious grieving asks a lot of us, but it is a valuable response to disenfranchisement. Instead of relying on an outside structure, we learn to create opportunities to mourn and celebrate our loved one's life. This is helpful for all of us to remember. Because even if you received support from the community, all losses ultimately become disenfranchised due to the passage of time. Friends and family live their own lives, forgetting the singular losses of one another. Losses fade into the background of our story, but they are still part of us. Every once in a while, on a certain date or with a gentle memory, we remember. We experience a STUG or a regret that stands alone in our new life. We return to feelings of loss and isolation. Social support is no longer available, but it is never too late for us to remember with love. It is never too late to enfranchise this new layer of grief through ritual or action on our own. In doing so, our movement toward healing renews and enriches the bonds of love we shared. We have learned that no one can judge the validity of another's tender experiences of loss. If our heart has felt loss, our grief will lead us to love.

Promptings of Hope

Twentieth-century Catholic mystic Thomas Merton writes in *A Book of Hours*, "Perhaps I am stronger than I think." As you claim your right to grieve, remember that even though you are suffering from the pain of loss, you have qualities and strengths that you can turn to in your healing. All of us can benefit from owning our grief and using creative ways to process our loss. As you explore ways to enfranchise your grief, embrace your feelings and let them guide you toward expression. Healing will follow as you enter and reenter your experience. If you let others know how wonderful your loved one was, you will find your heart filled with sweet memories of love. Here are some ideas that can be adapted to your individual circumstances. There is no time limit on creative grieving or reclaiming your feelings and your love.

- Invite folks over for your friend's birthday, make her favorite foods, and share stories that make you laugh and cry.

- Ask that your spouse be remembered in a worship service. Invite others to join the time of prayer, and follow up with a shared meal.

- Plan an event—golf tournament, pool party, potluck—anything that your coworker would have loved. Ask people to participate with donations to a favorite charity. Help her name be associated with a positive action in the world.

- Create a recipe book of her best dishes and give copies to family members.

- Write a poem for a special occasion or an ordinary day. Keep it to yourself or share it with another. His memory will be lifted up and your heart will be comforted.

CHAPTER 6

CREATING
YOUR OWN MAP

I magine that you are in a traffic jam. Your car is slowing down, and soon you will be stopping with nowhere to turn. Do you seek a side road? And once you make a commitment to an unknown road, do you think, "Well at least I'm moving—it's better than standing still"? The grieving process is similar to that. As you move down the main road of sadness, you can get bogged down in the traffic of doubt and fear or find a back road in order to keep moving. Sometimes your car breaks down, creating further complications. Grief has complications as well. Grief is unpredictable, with detours and pile-ups that are mostly out of our control. At the same time, we keep moving through it. The hard work of grief is cumulative. Everything helps us learn to navigate old roads, experiment with side trips, and explore new roads that lead to healing.

The territory of Passage is about motion, the ups and downs and back and forth of grief. We learn how to keep going, to keep moving through our experience of loss. Even when we pause to reflect on our feelings or return to a painful memory, the process of grief is still moving within us like an underground waterway beneath an ancient city. The movement of Passage may result in a return to Alone, where we bring new insights to old tasks and challenges. There is much to be learned, and we may stay in Passage longer than we like. Others who have studied and made this journey provide guidelines to identify the rhythms of grief. But we each create our own map. Grief can teach us resilience in response to loss and hope in response to despair.

THE BACK AND FORTH OF GRIEVING

Grief's unpredictability is one of our biggest challenges. We have no control over our emotions, other people, or the new world without our loved one in it. We seek order and we find chaos. We seek a logical progression and find constant change. Stage theory attempts to provide a linear structure for the fluid grief process. Based on the idea that elements in systems move through a distinct pattern, it can be comforting to see the unpredictability of grief corralled into a beginning, a middle, and, blessedly, an end. At the same time, it is misleading to rely upon discrete stages to explain grief. The process simply does not move in an orderly, linear path. Kenneth R. Mitchell and Herbert Anderson, authors of *All Our Losses, All Our Griefs: Resources for Pastoral Care*, explain it this way:

> If grief in any given instance is unique, it follows that it is unpredictable. The nature of our attachment to a person or object is formed without conscious awareness. It is therefore difficult to anticipate the intensity or complexity of grief. . . . Recognition of the unpredictability of grief leads to the realization that it is not useful to define grief in terms of stages except in the broadest possible way.[1]

Stage theory also sets us up to judge our progress in grief, and we can become discouraged when our experience differs from the prescribed stages. Or we think "I must be doing it wrong" when we "backtrack" to an earlier stage. We do not need to add these negative attitudes to our grief. It is difficult enough.

Let's turn instead to the wisdom and workings of our bodies to explain how grief helps us respond to loss. What does a parent do to calm a crying baby? Instinctively, he rocks the child back and forth, back and forth. Both baby and dad are calmed by the gentle swaying movement. Or how do we relax after a stressful meeting? We might practice deep breathing. The stress is diffused through slow, mindful in-breaths and out-breaths. Perhaps you've experienced the calming effect of a rocking chair or a playground swing. As human beings, we oscillate without even thinking about it. Our muscles tighten and then relax, our hearts beat rhythmically. We sleep and rise, moving back and forth between rest and activity. Oscillation is a natural response to the stress of life, helping us return to a balanced, more centered state.

According to current bereavement theory, grief is essentially a stress reaction to loss. It is a natural response to this one event that has interrupted our life and turned it upside down. Grief calls upon our inborn tendency toward oscillation, our natural rhythmic response, to assist us in finding relief. George Bonanno describes grief's oscillation in this way:

> Like any stress reaction, it is not uniform or static. Relentless grief would be overwhelming. Grief is tolerable, actually, only because it comes and goes in a kind of oscillation. We move back and forth emotionally. We focus on the pain of the loss, its implications, its meanings, and then our minds swing back toward the immediate world, other people, and what is going on in the present. We temporarily lighten up and reconnect with

those around us. Then we dive back down and continue the process of mourning.[2]

It is as if we have an inner gyroscope to help us navigate our loss, orienting us between two ways of coping with the pain. We enter the loss, allowing the feelings to exist, and then we reenter our lives, allowing daily life to ground us. This realistic explanation of how we grieve, known as the Dual Process Model (DPM) of coping with bereavement, incorporates our body's natural process for recovery. While the death of a loved one changes everything and relief seems impossible, it is also true that we usually find our way through loss. The oscillating rhythm of healing is inborn. Psychologists Margaret Stroebe and Henk Schut developed the DPM with this understanding of our human capacity for growth and recovery.

> The principle underlying oscillation is that at times the bereaved will confront aspects of loss, at other times avoid them, and the same applies to the tasks of restoration. Sometimes, too, there will be "time out," when the person is not grieving.[3]

Through the back and forth of grieving, we find relief. Oscillation's dynamic process pulls us out of and into loss and restoration as we heal. Grief researchers Cynthia L. Schultz and Darcy L. Harris explain that this flexible model of grief "describes the unfolding of one's grief experience as an oscillation between focus upon the relationship with the deceased individual (loss orientation) with an alternate focus upon tasks of everyday life and distractions (restoration orientation)."[4]

The loss-oriented responses to the stress of death include the most common emotional experiences associated with grief: sadness, loneliness, and the constant adjustment to life that this particular loss demands. We see the world through the lens of absence, which shapes our attitudes and behaviors. Loss-oriented coping includes withdrawing from social situations, sinking into memories, and staying focused on our feelings. Restoration-oriented coping, on the other hand, refers to our efforts to keep going, to stay focused on tasks, to find respite from grief's intrusion in our life. Here we try to live again. Restoration-oriented or restorative behaviors include making new friends or participating in a book group or cooking class. It can be restorative to sit down and address financial matters or to just go through the motions of daily life; such choices provide a distraction from the emotional demands of grieving.

Marion came to our bereavement support group reluctantly. Her husband's death was sudden and thrust her into a life she didn't want. She was sad and mad and could not believe that would ever change. Her stories revealed her resistance toward taking care of herself or trying new things, but she came each week. Somehow Marion gave herself permission to listen to others as she struggled with her own feelings. Our last session included a collage-making activity. Marion quietly chose pictures and words that described the state of her heart. As each group member shared their feelings and collage, we honored their hard work and courage. Marion looked around the circle as she held up her efforts and said, "All this time I thought I was coming to these meetings for Brian, but now I realize this is about me." In her own way, Marion moved back and forth between loss and restoration, discovering new feelings and a little bit of hope. She trusted others and the process, which allowed her to try out, for a time, another way to cope with her husband's death.

Some days we may doubt our capacity to heal from the pain of loss. When our feelings and the demands of life take hold, we can't imagine any long-term relief. We may ask ourselves, "Is it possible to survive this emotional roller coaster?" The back and forth of grieving is indeed unpredictable and intense, but at the same time it is a reliable reminder that our grieving is not static. It's movements are a reminder of the life within us that is leading us toward healing. As time passes, we learn to trust these shifts back and forth. We find ways to incorporate the rhythms of our grief into our lives. For some, it feels good to get back to work, to the new normal where they find new energy. Others, aware of sadness's return, might find themselves seeking the loss side of their bereavement. A son may play his dad's favorite piece of music and ride the oscillation right into a moment of tears. In this way, his dad is remembered and the son expresses his feelings. As we learn the ways of coping, we let them help us grieve. This understanding of bereavement asks us to trust the in and out of breathing and the back and forth of grieving.

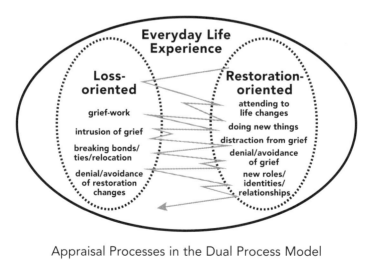

Appraisal Processes in the Dual Process Model

Source: Margaret Stroebe and Henk Schut, "The Dual Process Model of Coping with Bereavement: A Decade On," *OMEGA: Journal of Death and Dying* 61, no. 4 (2010): 273–89.

Promptings of Hope

"Often care of the soul means not taking sides when there is a conflict at a deep level. It may be necessary to stretch the heart wide enough to embrace contradiction and paradox." In *Care of the Soul*, psychotherapist and best-selling author Thomas Moore reminds you to look at the whole of your grief. The Dual Process Model does not stress one orientation over another. Instead, it honors your experience of both loss and restoration, as well as the journey between the two. The ups and downs, the ins and outs, of Passage provide a space to learn more about your own dual process as a resource for mapping your Land of Loss.

Using the diagram of the DPM as a reference, create your own list of loss-oriented and restoration-oriented behaviors and attitudes. Ask yourself, "What do I focus on when I face my loss?" Feelings, points of view, memories, expectations—all are fair game; no judgment. Then ask, "What do I focus on when I seek relief?" Hope, freedom from _____, responsibilities, peace of mind—all are possibilities; again, no judgment. Sit with your two lists, without interruption, and envision yourself moving back and forth between these two states of mind. What has that been like for you? Do you remember moments when grief pulled you one way or the other, without your permission? Perhaps you have memories of choosing a loss-oriented or a restorative behavior, even for a few minutes, to cope with your loss. Allow yourself to witness your own oscillation in the midst of your grief and consider the value of this inner wisdom as you continue to travel in the Land of Loss.

EXPERIMENTING WITH RESILIENCE

Herb's stories about his wife, Donna, and their life together were filled with warmth and tenderness. With tears in his eyes, he spoke about their love for one another and their children. At the same time, Herb laughed as he shared memories of a rain-soaked camping trip. Donna's illness had required long trips to an out-of-state hospital and extra effort to monitor her pain. Herb was grateful that he could take care of Donna and mentioned his faith in God as an important resource. He had expected her death, but had not expected the emptiness he was feeling. He kept repeating, "I'm just so grateful I had a chance to say goodbye, to tell her I loved her one more time."

Herb's emotions shift back and forth between the positive and the painful memories of his wife's illness and death. He has learned to be flexible with his feelings. Herb is not afraid of the sadness; he trusts it will pass someday. When he has a happy memory, he allows himself to feel the happiness without any guilt or regret attached. Herb finds relief, even peace, in those positive memories, and they are slowly helping him accept his new life without Donna. Through his emotional flexibility, Herb is experiencing resilience in his grief.

Hara Estroff Marano, editor at large for *Psychology Today*, says that "resilient people do not let adversity define them. They find resilience by moving toward a goal beyond themselves, transcending pain and grief by perceiving bad times as a temporary state of affairs."[5] This is not to suggest that Herb doesn't suffer. His wife's death and his daughters' subsequent sadness broke his heart. The demands of grief changed everything. At the same time, he learned to adapt to those changing demands and the stress of his loss. Herb knows that life is a good thing and keeps that awareness alive in the midst of his pain. As George Bonanno's intelligent study of resilience tells us,

Human beings are wired to survive. Not everybody manages well, but most do. And some of us, it seems, can deal with just about anything. We adapt, we change gears, we smile and laugh and do what we need to do, we nurture our memories, we tell ourselves it's not as bad as we thought, and before we know it, what once seemed bleak and bottomless has given way; the dark recedes and the sun once again peeks out from behind the clouds.[6]

How do we know what resiliency looks like? In general, resilient people:

- Find comfort in thinking about and speaking of their loved one
- Have a belief that life is good, that things are going to work out
- Refrain from blaming themselves when something is wrong
- Seek positive, life-giving relationships
- Adjust to changing demands of different situations
- Seek benefits instead of detriments, counting their blessings
- Believe in themselves and their ability to make choices

Some of the above may be familiar, comfortable, and already a part of who you are and how you handle adversity. Other aspects may be new or awkward, requiring a more experimental attitude. The Land of Loss is a place to take an honest look at your own resilient or not-so-resilient attitudes. Resilient characteristics can be cultivated and will help us with the challenges of loss. The first step is to return to our bodies and the wisdom they hold. We are indeed wired to adapt to change. The more we trust our body's physiological responses, the more we can work with and learn from our built-in resources to bounce back.

As Linda Graham, psychotherapist, neuroscience expert, and author of *Bouncing Back: Rewiring Your Brain for Maximum Resilience and Well-Being*, states,

> Resilience is the capacity to respond to pressures and tragedies quickly, adaptively, and effectively. Researchers have found that there is no single best or infallible way. Being able to adapt our coping to a specific challenge is the skill that allows us to find our footing when we're thrown off balance by the unknown, the stress, or by trauma.[7]

Graham explains that we learn resiliency through life events, relationships, and experimentation with coping strategies. Neuroscience shows that these coping strategies—and life—not only teach new behaviors but they also influence the actual brain structures that are doing the coping. Our brain's neuroplasticity, or adaptability at the cellular level, is an active, lifelong characteristic. This would suggest that our efforts to cultivate patience, for example, will train our brain to actually become more adept at being patient.

Graham's work suggests that when we intentionally develop brain functions to increase our resiliency, we add another resource for our grief-work. Since death has changed the shape and patterns of our lives forever, resilience training could help us find a more flexible response to that change. Her exercise "Hand on the Heart" is an example of the process and its physiological impact:

> Place your hand on your heart.
>
> *This physical touch, like a hug, offers a sense of calm and begins to release oxytocin, a hormone in the brain of safety and trust.*

Breathe gently, slow and deep breaths.

Slow, deep breathing will activate the parasympathetic nervous system, which also calms down the body and the mind.

Breathe into your heart any sense of goodness, safety, or trust you can muster.

Breathing positive emotions into the heart center will bring the heart rate variability back into a coherent rhythm.

Call to mind someone who loves you unconditionally, who you feel completely safe with. It could be your third-grade teacher, a spiritual figure, or even a pet. Savor the feeling of warmth, safety, and love in your body. When that feeling is steady, let go of the image and bathe in the warm glow for thirty seconds.

Research has shown that staying centered on this feeling of love and trust will further activate oxytocin, with its comfort of bonding and attachment, safety, and connection.[8]

With exercises like these, Linda Graham uses a form of self-directed neuroplasticity to create new neurons and neural pathways—that is, to help train our brains to recover from the stress of loss more comfortably. Resiliency training can play an important role in the Land of Loss. The map that you are creating is bound to include backtracking, detours, and redirection. That is the nature of travel and of grief. With a fluid, resilient attitude, we learn to make adjustments and adapt more easily. Resiliency helps create a path out of the pain. Upcoming events that may trigger painful feelings can be planned for or even perceived differently when we trust our capacity for resilience. We may seek positive, hopeful people to remind us of our own hope and desire for life. Even in the midst of sadness, seeds of resiliency can be planted through a practice of deep breathing to strengthen us as we take our very next steps.

Promptings of Hope

Marcel Proust tells us in *In Search of Lost Time* that "The only true voyage of discovery . . . would be not to visit strange lands but to possess other eyes, to behold the universe through the eyes of another, of a hundred others, to behold the hundred universes that each of them beholds, that each of them is." Grief's call to transformation encourages looking at things in new ways—if not with new eyes, at least with new glasses. This is a time to try things on, so to speak, to slip into new thoughts and behaviors and check them out. That's the beauty of experimenting. It is a process of exploration.

You are learning that your body is your ally in grief. Bring awareness to your hardworking body. If you have not tried yoga before, this could be the time to learn how to move in a new way. Local classes, Internet videos, and television classes can all provide reliable instruction on yoga poses. Some poses, like the Warrior, will encourage strength and dignity. Other poses will guide you through the process of holding and releasing tension. All forms of intentional movement, such as tai chi, Pilates, dancing, gentle stretching, and Rosen movement, can become a doorway into learning about and loving your body. As your body settles into new ways to move, your awareness will shift as well. Feelings and thoughts move in new directions. Let your body guide you to yourself.

PART 3

Surrender

Many travelers have seen the signs that point toward the Cliffs of Uncertainty and said to themselves, "Maybe there is another way." The cliffs stand high above the trail and require a consistent effort to ascend. Standing at the edge, travelers have a chance to catch their breath as they look back at their long journey and ahead into the unknown. The Cliffs of Uncertainty are a unique experience of trust, stepping off them calls upon new layers of courage and faith.

Surrender is a doorway into relying upon, returning to, or discovering our spiritual nature. This leap of faith is not limited to religious imagery; instead, it extends into a terrain that can be described as the fullness of love. Sometimes we call out as Catholic theologian Henri Nouwen did: "Dear God, I am so afraid to open my fists! Who will I be when I have nothing left to hold on to? Who will I be when I stand before you with empty hands?"[1] At other times, we understand that the love shared with those who died opens our hearts to a love that has been here all along. Love speaks through many languages; our "letting go" in Surrender helps us hear the message meant for *our* heart, for *our* loss.

J. William Worden encourages us to "adjust to a world without the deceased" in it. Surrender's lessons of stepping into fear and admitting powerlessness prepare us for this task as we let go into love's tender care. Our eyes are opened to the gifts of love that come our way through nature, caring people, challenges, and acts of compassion. Our hearts are tuned to the frequency of love in the present moment. Surrender's call may feel scary; our fears and feelings of powerlessness can be overwhelming. Navigating this region of loss "requires enormous psychic strength," Francis Weller explains. "For us to tolerate the images, emotions, memories, and dreams that arise in times of grief, we need to fortify our interior ground."[2] But the assurances of love gather around us, leading us home. Sister Doris Klein reminds us, "We must remember that to own the light is not to deny the darkness but to allow it to be transformed—and it takes courage to be faithful to this transformative process."[3]

CHAPTER 7

A COURAGEOUS CHOICE

While we have traveled far in the Land of Loss, there is more for us to learn. We may realize that fears lie beneath the sadness of our grief, and they too await our attention. Fear is our teacher, and we can choose how we respond to the lessons taught: with resistance or with courage. The choice is ours to make. As Alan Wolfelt states, "Actually, surrendering to the unknowable mystery is a courageous choice, an act of faith, a trust in God and in ourselves! We can only hold this mystery in our hearts and surround ourselves with love."[1]

This region in the Land of Loss also asks that we confront our ultimate powerlessness. We turn to the wisdom of recovery, as outlined by the twelve steps of Alcoholics Anonymous, to admit our powerlessness and seek support from a Higher Power. With intention and courage, we trust the ever-deepening experience of grieving as a pathway to love.

COMING TO KNOW OUR FEARS

Everything has changed. Everything ahead of us is unknown or will be impacted by the unknown. For some of us, this powerful experience of not knowing stirs up old fears relating to a sense of security or creates new ones focusing on this difficult moment in our life. We may experience fear regarding tangible concerns following the death: day-to-day life without our loved one in it or the loss of a caregiver or fear of facing other life circumstances in such a vulnerable state. Or we may be haunted by intangible concerns and unnamed fears that lie beneath the surface, unseen but present in our everyday experience.

One common example of an unnamed fear is the fear of our emotions themselves. We experience a range of profound emotional swings in grief, particularly in the early days of loss. We travel into dark places of despair and anguish, where we feel out of control. Without realizing it, we try to repress these powerful and painful feelings, but they are there, lurking behind the scenes as reminders of our ultimate vulnerability. Some people feel that if they allow themselves to be sad or mad, the feeling will never stop. They fear the rest of their life will be defined by these dark emotions over which they have no control. As psychotherapist Miriam Greenspan explains,

> The fear of falling into the darkness, of going down and not being able to come up, lurks right at the edge of our ability to feel at all. Like a child who locks the closet door in terror of the monster inside, the more we lock up our dark emotions, the more we fear that they'll jump out of the closet and devour us.[2]

Christine's adult daughter, Kathy, died after a painful struggle with breast cancer. When Christine looked at the two young sons and devoted fiancé that Kathy left behind, she felt her sadness turn into rage: "How can they grow up without knowing their mother? Why did she have to suffer?" But Christine, like many of us, was afraid of her anger and its power. As she privately managed the dark stirrings inside, she felt her body tighten, and she watched herself withdraw from her family. Christine feared that, once unleashed, anger would emerge in other areas of her life, too. She believed that her relationships, self-image, and attitude toward life were all in danger from anger's negative influence. Christine feared being defined, perhaps judged, as an "angry woman." She thought it was easier to keep a lid on her anger and ignore its efforts to get her attention.

When confronted with loss, some people fear that their spiritual beliefs and explanations of death are inadequate. Childhood teachings no longer bring comfort or clarity, and adult spirituality feels insufficient. We may accept that our living connection to our loved one is gone, but we want something in its place. We want to trust that a lasting spiritual connection is possible. Grief forces some of us to confront our belief system, sometimes with doubt right alongside. We may fear that this difficult path before us is God's choosing, that God "took away" our loved one and ignored our pleas for their recovery. Or we may decide there is no God and no meaning in this tragedy. To sort out what we truly believe about death and the Divine, we may have to align with or reject a long-held point of view, creating further confusion.

Mary's upbringing did not include belief in God, religious education, or family prayer. In her adult years, she mocked believers and relied upon her intellect to make sense of life. But after her mother died, Mary was confronted with an experience that changed everything for her. Her mother had moved in with Mary and her husband, to be cared for as she declined from cancer. That was difficult, but Mary has never regretted the opportunity to actively love her mother at the end of her life. Following the death, Mary had an experience that filled her with a sense of calm and peace unlike anything she had ever known. Her grief included anguish and sadness, and, at the same time, she was aware of a presence of love that was unexplainable but real. She started reading about those who have encountered Mystery, including Thomas Merton's autobiography, *Seven Storey Mountain*, and found language that explained what she had felt. It became clear to Mary that her mother's death was followed by a moment of grace. She made the decision to keep an open mind toward God's place in her life, trusting a new path in her grief.

It is also common to fear the unpredictable process of grief. As a result, many of us respond to loss as we respond to life, turning grief into a problem to be solved, a challenge to be met, or an accomplishment to be achieved. Instead of treating our own grief as we might treat a neighbor or coworker's grief, with patience and gentleness, we place demands on ourselves. Our fear tries to manage the unpredictability of grief, which leads to added and unneeded pressure. The healing nature of grief that honors our needs, our personality, and our heart is lost.

RESPONSE TO FEAR—RESISTANCE OR COURAGE

It is normal to avoid painful emotions and deny the fears that lie deep within. Our resistance often happens without us thinking about it, but if we are to move toward recovery it is helpful to untangle some of the particulars. Fear's presence, for example, can intensify the feelings of sadness, anger, or despair that accompany normal grief. Fears can be unreasonable and have great power over us. They become overwhelming when we begin to fear—as Franklin D. Roosevelt said—fear itself. Our resistance then becomes an unconscious reaction to baffling sensations that creep into our thoughts and feelings. Our individual fears may remain nameless, even though naming them would help defuse their power. Without resources such as personal wisdom, spiritual belief, professional support, or a faith tradition, fears can grow.

A more conscious resistance occurs when we actively deny our feelings. Some of us believe that it is better to stay strong in the face of emotional challenges. We may rely upon an artificial strength to protect ourselves from pain. This impetus to resist normal fears has merit, of course; the demands of life do not stop because of our grief. We need time away from the sadness, for example, to address quotidian tasks and responsibilities. But resistance to grief can become a pattern that denies the individual the space to accept and process what is happening on an emotional level. It does not help that our Western culture sends the message to "get over it" or to pull ourselves up by our bootstraps and move on. When we move away from the deep rhythms of our human experience, we no longer honor the human complexities uncovered by grief, including the roots of our fears.

Remember, our efforts to avoid or resist fear do not have a fine-tuning capability. When we place barriers around difficult feelings, the more pleasant feelings can be swept into the dark, along with fear and other sources of pain. This can lead to a numbing of all our emotions and a limiting of our connections to the fullness of life. If we avoid or resist the fears associated with our grief, we focus on survival at the expense of healing. Rabbi Elie Kaplan Spitz tells us,

> When we experience loss, the injury may leave us more compromised than before. Life can weaken us, leaving us in pain, exhausted, and self-pitying, when we are carrying beyond our capacity. . . . Our unaddressed resentment is expressed as hostility, violence, and isolation. The longer we carry the weight of unexamined losses, the heavier they become.[3]

The paradox of Surrender is that the strength we seek to step into our fear is found within our willingness to be vulnerable. Its name is courage. Like spiritual journeys and traditions across time and around the world, grief calls us into the Mystery, where courage resides. "The way of surrender is the way of the mystics, of the dark night of the soul, of the descent of Isis into the underworld, of being wracked upon the wheel of pain and returning transformed," writes Miriam Greenspan.[4] We may fear life without our loved one in it, and yet that is the life before us. We may have lost confidence in our capacity to choose and function, and still we must. Our fear of the unknown is a reasonable response to loss. At the same time, each small step we take will help us stay on the path of healing. Each time we share our feelings with a friend or attend a program to learn more about grief, we are choosing courage. Our surrender to our fears and to grief's course through the Land of Loss leads us toward stable ground.

J. William Worden's third task of mourning seems to mirror one of the fears we might be facing. He tells us "to adjust to a world without the deceased." We may look back at the adjustments made so far and shout, "No! I cannot change anymore!" The adjustments you have made can be overwhelming, but remember, they are yours to make. As you untangle the fears you have and the lessons they teach, have confidence in how far you have come. Trust the wisdom that has brought you to this place. While discussing the third task, Worden adds, "[You] will be quite capable of making decisions and taking actions when [you] are ready and . . . not make decisions just to reduce the pain."[5] The strength you seek to survive grief's demands is not found in resistance but within the tenderness of your loving heart.

FEAR AS A RESOURCE IN GRIEF

Our fears serve as a call to growth. Personal growth is not a priority for a newly grieving person. But, as time passes, our journey teaches us about trusting ourselves and trusting our process of grief. We are being led to the deepest part of ourselves. As we humbly confront our limitations, our fears remind us that we are human. Admitting our fear does not define who we are but rather illuminates who we are becoming.

As Christine (whose daughter died of breast cancer) experimented with her grieving, she chose to step into her fear and express her anger. She wrote a letter to cancer, then read it out loud, surrendering to the intense emotion she was feeling. With a loud, angry voice, Christine told cancer about the damage it had done. She did not waver as she expressed her feelings. Later, she was inspired to burn the letter and then she ceremoniously sent the black ashes down the garbage disposal. She bravely followed her instincts and claimed her anger at this outrageous end to her beautiful daughter's life. She didn't hold back, but spoke her truth, through word and action, without fear.

What happened next surprised her. The world did not collapse. She was not punished for expressing her deep, painful feelings. She did not suddenly turn into an angry person. Instead, something shifted in her heart and she felt an inner calm. Not long after, while using an onion chopper for that night's dinner, Christine felt a surge of energy that led her to push faster and harder on the chopper's knob. She was aware that her anger had returned, and she allowed herself to experience it once again. Before too long, the onion became a puddle of white liquid on the cutting board. Looking down at the puddle, Christine experienced a degree of satisfaction, both in the onion's transformation and in her own. She stepped into her fear when she acknowledged and expressed her anger. In doing so, Christine was released from an experience of helplessness in her grief into one of empowerment. She claimed her memories of her daughter and the love that they shared, bringing them with her as she healed. Miriam Greenspan describes fear and other dark emotions as a doorway into such moments of healing and transformation:

> These dark emotions are in-the-body energies, mediated by beliefs we have gathered from the culture of family and society around us. Their purpose is not to make us miserable, drive us crazy, or shame, weaken, or defeat us, but to teach us about ourselves, others, and the world, to open our hearts to compassion, to help us heal, and to change our lives. They bring us information and supply us with energy—the raw material of spiritual empowerment and transformation. When we know how to listen to them, we can ride their energy like a wave, with awareness as our protection. Emotional energy flows and a hidden doorway in the heart opens. Something shifts. A transmutation occurs: a movement through pain to spiritual power.[6]

Our fears ask us to look at questions of survival, identity, and spirituality. These facets of our story may have never received our attention, but if we are to go forward, we must consider our response to them. The choice to step into our fear becomes a pathway for life as well as grief. Each time we say yes to our fears and vulnerabilities, we move closer to our hopes and strengths. Brené Brown describes it this way:

> Owning our story can be hard but not nearly as difficult as spending our lives running from it. Embracing our vulnerabilities is risky but not nearly as dangerous as giving up on love and belonging and joy—the experiences that make us the most vulnerable. Only when we are brave enough to explore the darkness will we discover the infinite power of our light.[7]

As we draw upon and cultivate courage, we explore who we are becoming. We learn to travel slowly and gently, for this is sacred ground. This brave response to our fear has the potential to lead us into another journey—one that transcends grief and leads us into the greater mystery of Divine Love. With increased hope and awareness, it is possible to experience an ongoing connection with our loved one. A connection that is not limited to an ache when it's mentioned, but one that lives as a source of strength, hope, and life.

HOW DO WE LEARN FROM OUR FEAR?

In order to learn from our fear, we begin with great respect for fear's role in our story. As unconscious coping mechanisms, our fears protect us in the midst of loss, challenge, and chaos. They keep us safe, help build our confidence, and let us know what is important to us. Our fear is not an enemy, but more an overprotective big brother or sister.

So first it is important to respect and befriend your fear. Pay attention to thoughts or bodily sensations that you have been ignoring, as they may be forms of fear. Each may be speaking, and your job is to listen. Practice deep breathing and trust your body's wisdom. Place your hand on your chest and wait. Do you experience a heaviness in your chest or a nagging thought that will not leave? Do you find yourself avoiding talking about your feelings? Do you toss and turn in bed or keep yourself exceptionally busy? It is possible that fear is trying to get your attention.

As life goes forward with its constant stream of demands and activity, keep a door open to this new relationship with your fear. There is no rush to this kind of work; let it evolve in its own way. Take a deep breath and write down what you are experiencing. Just be with it. The process is a gentle one, with a time line all its own. Let your lived experience untangle, and let your awareness diminish the fear. Listen carefully and try to name the fear that waits to be known—fear of your limitations, fear of your strengths, fear of an uncharted future, fear of loss of control, fear of loneliness, fear of being happy. And remember, no judgment and no agenda, just listening.

This is a process of surrender, yes, but not in the sense of losing on a battlefield and waving a white flag. It is not the surrender of admitting you are wrong, as our dualistic culture would suggest. Surrender in the Land of Loss is a matter of allowing our heart, mind, and body to come into alignment with one another and with life all around us. We stop resisting our feelings and let them be heard and felt. When we can do that in an intentional, mindful way, we courageously move toward healing.

Osho, a spiritual teacher in the Hindu tradition, put it this way: "The way of the heart is the way of courage. It is to live in insecurity; it is to live in love, and trust; it is to move in the unknown. It is leaving the past and allowing the future to be. Courage is to move on dangerous paths."[8] We know the danger Osho speaks of, the painful adaptations that our trails through the Land of Loss have required. At the same time, as we courageously embrace our fear, we experience more compassion for ourselves and for others. We step into the deep and encounter love.

Promptings of Hope

"You have to grow from the inside out. None can teach you, none can make you spiritual. There is no other teacher but your own soul." In *Pearls of Wisdom*, Vivekananda, a Hindu mystic from the late 1800s, affirms the unique and sometimes lonely path we are on. Yet we are not without hope. This "growing" that Vivekananda speaks of is the force of life within each of us. It is no different from a delicate orchid opening to the light or the complex root system that connects one redwood to the next. The orchid, the redwood family, and our wounded hearts each have their own path toward maturity. Each has an intrinsic beauty and strength that sustains the journey.

Some of our fears are more obvious than others. Before traveling in deep waters, take some time to get to know the fears that have already shown up. If you lost your spouse, for example, you may fear taking on his or her role in the household. You may believe you can never do it correctly. You may fear that as you try to plan a vacation or negotiate with the car salesman you will be erasing his or her place in your life. Look at the moments of pause or resistance with curiosity. They are there to teach you about your growing edges. Do not react as a moment of fear appears. Instead, ask it what it is trying to tell you about yourself. Ask questions if you like, and trust the answers. Let your dialogue with fear defuse its hold on your brave and beautiful heart.

Admit Powerlessness

Most of us make plans, gather what we need to accomplish them, and then follow through. Whether we are parenting a small child, running a business, going grocery shopping, or selling real estate, we all follow this basic pattern. Even a retired person with access to larger amounts of time creates a structure for daily life. When we seek to establish control in our lives, and often our relationships, we come to believe that we actually *have* control—until a crisis occurs.

We, who have experienced the death of someone we love, have learned this in a very personal, painful way. Suddenly, we discover that we have no control over anything. Illness, pain, accidents, or violence have led to death, and we couldn't stop any of it. Now, as we grieve, we must admit that we had no control over our arrival in the Land of Loss as well. We were thrust into the emptiness of Alone and slogged our way through the lessons of Passage, often unwillingly, but we kept moving. Grief has been our guide and our teacher as we relearn and re-create our lives. Hopefully we've come to trust the process and believe it helps heal the wounds of loss. With each step taken, we've made the choice to increase our awareness and our active participation in the journey. Moving toward deeper healing, the reminder of our powerlessness returns.

Surrender presents a unique landscape where the "both/and" of our grief becomes more evident. When we gathered resources in Alone, we discussed holding sadness and hope at the same time. In Passage, nondual awareness emerged from grief's anguish and taught us to accept the moments of peace that coexist alongside such deep sadness. Surrender's lessons of powerlessness are also conveyed through nonduality. Mindfulness speaker and author Heather Stang explains it this way:

[Mindfulness] means shifting from an "either/or" point of view to the inclusive state of "and," or what some teachers describe as a "this, too" state of mind. When you learn to make this gradual shift you will be on your way to freeing yourself from what feels like an endless cycle of suffering, and while pain will still exist, you will come to learn that just like pleasure, suffering too is impermanent.[9]

We are assured of Surrender's safe, patient environment as this awareness unfolds. We might experience nudges and shifts into a more profound acceptance of change, asking our-selves, "Can I bear to imagine my life without him or her in it?" or "If I stop holding on to the pain, will I lose the only con-nection I have?" But we do not need to answer these questions right away. Instead, our choice becomes a time of residence in Surrender's cocoon, a place of waiting and transformation. Our powerlessness becomes our teacher.

Grief and the Twelve Steps

Alcoholics Anonymous is a well-established source of wisdom about powerlessness. Over two million people worldwide have found support and recovery in the overwhelming experience of addiction. William DeJong, a social psychologist and lecturer in alcohol addiction at the Harvard School of Public Health, says the success of AA can be measured by the number of other self-help groups that have imitated it. The Twelve-Step Recovery Program asks addicts, alcoholics, codependents, and others with addictive behaviors, "Are you willing to admit your powerlessness? Are you willing to trust a power greater than yourself to stay clean or sober?" AA's step-by-step process is an invitation to surrender into a more authentic relationship with oneself, with the place of struggle, and with one's Higher Power.

While grief is not the life-and-death issue that drugs and alcohol are, we who grieve are confronting a life-changing transition. How do we move into a new way of living and what are we leaving behind? Are we willing to trust a power greater than ourselves to help with the pain of loss? The Twelve Steps provide a template for the unique experience in Surrender, as we confront our inability to protect ourselves from loss and change. Bill W., the cofounder of Alcoholics Anonymous, "discovered two core principals of recovery. First, admit the problem, powerlessness over alcohol (and other drugs). Second, open up to a solution, a 'Higher Power,' any source of help outside yourself. These principles are, in essence, the first three steps in AA."[10] Our exploration of Twelve-Step wisdom will center on the first three steps as core sources of support we can choose for our grief recovery as well. As written in the Big Book, they are:

STEP ONE: We admitted we were powerless over alcohol—that our lives had become unmanageable.

STEP TWO: Came to believe that a power greater than ourselves could restore us to sanity.

STEP THREE: Made a decision to turn our will and our lives over to God as we understood Him.[11]

The unfolding of these steps provides gentle but clear navigation through powerlessness and, with some minor adjustments, provides access to our surrender in grief. Others have adopted Twelve-Step wisdom. Emotions Anonymous, for example, translated the steps to support those who are powerless over their emotions. A variety of fellowships, such as Debtors Anonymous and Workaholics Anonymous, have been patterned after the Twelve Steps. Our translation, for use in the Land of Loss, offers one more tool for our ongoing journey.

STEP ONE: WE ADMIT WE ARE POWERLESS OVER LOSS, THAT WE CANNOT CONTROL EVENTS AND EMOTIONS FOLLOWING A DEATH.

Some of us put pressure on ourselves, still thinking we could have done something to prevent the death, or at least be better at grieving by now. Some of us put our whole body on alert to resist this layer of acceptance. But as psychologist and religious educator Wayne Edward Oates explains,

> Grief is not a test of "how much you can take it." The test is the loss of all strength. Something has happened over which you had no control. You have never been so aware of your weakness, helplessness, and powerlessness. Nor have you ever been less willing to admit it to yourself.[12]

Step One's invitation, to admit our powerlessness over loss, is a call to acknowledge our deeply rooted vulnerability. When we choose to make that admission, it is as if a wise part of ourselves reaches out to hold our hurt and angry self by the hand. We turn and look at what happened, reassure ourselves, and then slowly lead ourselves toward surrender. In *Recovery—the Sacred Art: The Twelve Steps as Spiritual Practice*, rabbi and theologian Rami Shapiro explains,

> At its deepest, Step One is not saying we are powerless over some things and powerful over others. It is saying we are powerless over life itself. Life is not something we control or manage. Life is something that happens to us, in us, and through us. We respond to what life brings; we do not control what it brings.[13]

Certainly that is the case in the face of death—we do not and cannot control anything. We are truly vulnerable. It is worth remembering, especially on the precipice of Surrender, that the soft, vulnerable place inside us is the doorway into the best of who we are. It is worth our care and attention. In Alone, we learned to see vulnerability as a resource, but our long travels through the Land of Loss might have re-hardened our defenses around such tenderness. As we admit our powerlessness, it is important to remember, as Miriam Greenspan writes,

> Vulnerability is not just about hurting. It is about openness. Not only to pain, adversity, loss, and death, but also to the things we most desire and cherish: to love, intimacy, creativity, sex, birth, wonder: to being truly touched by another human being, being truly seen for who we are; to the sheer advantage of being alive; to the sacred spirit that imbues the world.[14]

Greenspan speaks with the wisdom of a professional psychotherapist, as well as of a mother who described the death of
her infant son, in her book *Healing through the Dark Emotions:
The Wisdom of Grief, Fear and Despair*. She goes on to explain,
"When we are most vulnerable, we are most alive, most open
to all the dimensions of existence."[15]

This is the mystery of our powerlessness and the path to
healing. When we admit we are powerless over loss and that
we cannot control the events and emotions following a death,
we leave behind the expectations that can never be fulfilled.
Instead of the anguish of longing, we move into a new space
of waiting. What are we waiting for? We don't know yet.
Still, the Twelve Steps move us toward an ever-deepening
layer of trust.

STEP TWO: CAME TO BELIEVE THAT A POWER GREATER THAN OURSELVES COULD RESTORE OUR INNER WISDOM WITHIN THE CHAOS OF LOSS.

When we admit our powerlessness in the first step, it can feel
as if we are adrift at sea. We realize we have lost our mooring
and our connection to a safe harbor. Step Two then asks us to
acknowledge that we need help. Before we have even identified our greater power, we are being asked to admit we need
one! This humble path, as Rabbi Shapiro describes it, is "the
ability to admit that when it comes to the core questions about
who you are and why you are here on this planet, the only honest answer is, 'I don't know.'"[16] We do not know such answers
about ourselves. We do not know why someone we loved had
to die or why our grief is so painful. Some of us do not know
a power greater than ourselves, but Step Two asks us to risk
a humble look beyond our fears and resistance. We are being
invited to consider and choose spiritual paths for healing.

Many of us resist the idea of surrendering to God. It challenges our sense of autonomy and independence. Some of us

are angry at God or any power that would cause pain. Since we carried that anger throughout our grief, we have experienced its influence on our life and relationships. Whatever our path, we stand before the inescapable truth of a new life before us. What if Surrender is an invitation to step into life with love, not loss, as our companion? Can we open our heart to the possibility of life and allow access for love's healing to enter our deepest places?

When we relinquish control to a power greater than ourselves, we enter sacred ground. We restore an inner connection that has been within us all along, though we might not have words for it. As John E. Welshons comments,

> [We return to] moments when everything seemed "okay," when our instinctive trust in the Universe came to the surface and we let down our guard and defenses. We felt warmth, we felt peace, we felt contentment. We breathed in deeply, our shoulders uncharacteristically low. . . . The subtle fear was gone. The wariness melted. . . . We felt connected. We felt complete. We felt whole.[17]

Welshons offers these clues to describe the "state of expansiveness" that many call love; others may call it God. It's been waiting for us, peeking out through a feeling of oneness with nature or of a return to our mother's arms. Or we know it as "the experience we were born for . . . the 'peace that passeth all understanding.'"[18] We experience such peace through different moments: childbirth, artistic endeavors, mountain climbing, lovemaking, or scientific breakthroughs. Our humanity reminds us, over and over, of love's tender touch entering our consciousness when we pray, stare at the night sky, lean into curves on a motorcycle, sit by a stream, or hear another say "I love you." Welshons adds, "At these moments, we transcend our limitations. And the state of expansiveness we move into is love." Could our surrender to loss teach us to surrender to healing waves of love?

Step Two's call requires a receptive heart that suggests, as grief recovery coach Jeannie Ewing explains, a type of "spiritual nakedness, an openness and purposeful exposure of heart that is visible to both God and others."[19] When our hearts remain open to the possibility of power beyond our own, we are invited to come back "home."

STEP THREE: MADE A DECISION TO TURN OUR LOSS OVER TO GOD AS WE UNDERSTOOD GOD.

Step Three asks us to make a choice: to embrace a personal understanding of the Divine. "Step Three invites you to become your own theologian," Rami Shapiro reminds us, "to create an idea of God that allows you to trust in something greater than yourself."[20] Those of us who have a defined and comfortable experience with the Divine can find rest in that relationship. Others of us may have questions or resentment toward the God we had relied upon.

As your own theologian, this is the time to sort out your feelings about, and your relationship with, God. Let the God of your understanding know how you feel. Ask for what you need. Bring all your sadness, fear, anger, and confusion into the conversation. The more real you are, the more real your relationship will be.

As we grieve, our fears or doubts may return, but Step Three asks us to trust our sacred connection, or as Rami Shapiro puts it, to "fall into the arms of God." This is the language of surrender, inviting us into a loving embrace that will carry our grief. Through this step, we no longer measure grief by days or months. Instead, we are guided to "let go and let God," with love lighting the way.

For some of us, a reliance upon a Higher Power becomes a roadblock. Our concept of God is unclear or absent, or our own experience of "spirit" does not fit within a religious landscape. Some of us cannot reconcile dependence on a Higher Power. But as AA suggests:

> Every modern house has electric wiring carrying power and light to its interior. We are delighted with this dependence; our main hope is that nothing will ever cut off the supply of current. By so accepting our dependence upon this marvel of science, we find ourselves more independent personally. Not only are we more independent, we are even more comfortable and secure. Power flows just where it is needed.[21]

Our desire to heal from the pain of loss might be the impetus to surrender former attitudes toward spirituality and, perhaps experimentally, access some of that hidden "power," by whatever name we call it.

In *Waiting: A Nonbeliever's Higher Power*, author Marya Hornbacher shares that "listening for spirit is a complicated process when we do not believe in a God or do not feel a connection to what may be a Higher Power. Many of us have been trained to think of 'spirituality' as the sole provenance of religion."[22] Her journey of recovery from grief and alcoholism allowed her to move through her doubts and find her own language for the Divine, her own Higher Power.

> When I speak of spirit, I am not speaking of something related to or given by a force outside ourselves. I am speaking of a force that is ourselves. The experience of living in the world, bound by a body, space and time, woven into the connection of human history, human

connection and human life. This is the force that feels and thinks and gives us consciousness at all; it is our awareness of presence in the world. It is the deepest, most elemental, most integral part of who we are; it is who we are.[23]

Your journey through the aloneness and chaos of loss, your feelings of despair and anger, and your arrival at this moment in your grief have brought you, too, to the "deepest, most elemental, most integral part" of who you are. Instead of something to avoid or deny, perhaps this vulnerable experience is your doorway into the healing that you seek. Perhaps your grief is leading you home. This is not easy. The journey through the Land of Loss and the steps require, as Hornbacher writes, "a careful and intensive look inward, a deepening knowledge of ourselves, our actions, and our beliefs, so that we can be more intimately, spiritually connected to the world in which we live. [The Steps] ask us to take that look inward, and ultimately bring us to a spiritual wholeness where we have the capacity to love and serve the world outside our limited selves."[24]

Promptings of Hope

"We must believe in the value of that inner road and trust that it will lead us to places in the heart that are waiting to bless us with their truth and beauty." Sister Joyce Rupp's reminder in *Praying Our Goodbyes* offers hope in the confusing places of powerlessness. May her words help you respond to each of these steps and make them your own.

Explore this progression of surrender through the first three steps as you think about your own grief process. Take it slowly; write about one step at a time. If possible, give yourself permission to write about specific words or phrases that you wish to challenge or seek deeper understanding of. Use your work as a palette to explore your relationship with Twelve-Step wisdom and your own powerlessness over loss.

Step One: We admit we are powerless over loss, that we cannot control the events and emotions following a death.

Step Two: Believe that a power greater than ourselves could restore our inner wisdom within the chaos of loss.

Step Three: Made a decision to turn our loss over to God as we understood God.

CHAPTER 8

LETTING GO
INTO LOVE

Surrender is a land of letting go, a place where we relax our
grip on what could have been or what should be. Instead,
we make space for what is. For most of us, this is a challenging task. We are usually laden with expectations. We expect
life to unfold in a certain way or relationships to meet our
needs. Loss has intensified our human longing and turned our
unmet expectations into further painful evidence of what is
not to be. As we take the brave steps deeper into our healing,
however, we move into an acceptance that changes us. We live
out of our vulnerability and encounter a certain tenderness
that becomes our strength. We shift away from control into
empowerment, away from isolation into love.

Sister Doris Klein, artist and spiritual director, uses art to
speak of these human movements toward wholeness. In her
book *Journey of the Soul*, a rainbow-colored figure stands with
arms raised, surrounded and penetrated by light. Sister Doris
describes the moment:

> The grace of surrender asks us to relax into the Mystery,
> to acknowledge that we cannot walk alone in this place.

> Rather than assume a stance of defeat, we ask to be embraced by a Love that is greater than the confusion, pain, or frustration we are experiencing. . . . Once we accept in our heart the truth of being loved, we loosen our grip on control and are surprisingly free to act in integrity and light.[1]

This is our journey as well, for this moment in our grief asks us to trust the Divine Love that surrounds and holds our grieving heart. We are asked to trust not only that will we be okay, but also that we will find new purpose and learn to love in new ways.

Conscious grieving risks everything—memories, identity, connections—as we trust a new way of being. We have struggled with the shock of our aloneness and the confusion of processing our pain. Now with new eyes, we see the gift of life around us—the natural world, companions on the trail, uplifting messages, and the hand of God. As Francis Weller explains, "Grief pulls us into the underworld, where we are invited to discover a new mode of seeing, one that reveals the holiness of all things."[2]

LOVE IN THE PRESENT MOMENT

One of the greatest fears in the journey through grief is losing our special connection with this one person. Many of us believe, "If I accept his death, if I truly let go, I will lose him. Forever." At the same time, everything inside us knows they are physically gone. Forever. As bereavement psychologist Dennis Klass writes, our grief is a process of moving from "equilibrium in [our] inner and social worlds before a death to new equilibrium following bereavement. Equilibrium is difficult to measure, but easy to sense subjectively."[3] So we try things on, attitudes and beliefs, to see what fits as our new life evolves. We might ask ourselves, "Okay, if I fully accept tht *he* is gone, what happens to the love we shared? Where does *that* go?"

This is a fair question. Love seems to come alive when we are in each other's presence. After death, when shared physical presence is no longer possible, our hearts stretch and stretch further to reclaim the feeling that was like no other. Episcopal priest and theologian Cynthia Bourgeault tells us that when we mourn "We are in a state of free fall, our heart reaching toward what we have seemingly lost but cannot help loving anyway. To mourn is to live between the realms."[4] Or, one might say, to mourn is to live between the past, the present, and the future. From this perspective, we might ask a new question: Is it possible to remember that unique experience of shared love we had in the past and, at the same time, stay open to the possibility of other forms of love in the present? Can we accept the both/and of our grief? Bourgeault responds:

> If we can remain open, we discover a mysterious "something" does indeed reach back to comfort us; the tendrils of our grief trailing out into the unknown become intertwined in a greater love that holds things together. To mourn is to touch directly the substance of divine compassion. And just as ice must melt before it can begin to flow, we, too, must become liquid before we can flow into the larger mind.[5]

There is no time line to the sacred art of grieving. In fact, as we bring our focus to the present moment, time seems to slow down. We learn to respect the rhythms of our grief in the Land of Loss and, as psychologists Richard G. Tedeschi and Lawrence G. Calhoun describe, we see that "Losses can be mourned even as positive changes become evident."[6] At one point, we embrace the nondual thinking that allows our sadness and hope to coexist, becoming more accepting of life's complexities. Or, we experiment with a new relationship with our loved one. We try out one that transcends physical presence, turning to a connection of heart and spirit. At the same time, we might step back into our pain to complete unfinished business in our grief. This time, Stephen Levine suggests, we might "enter [the pain] with mercy, instead of walling it off with fear. . . . Let what seems an improbable love—the ultimate acceptance of our pain—enter the cluster of sensations that so agitate the mind and body."[7]

When Sam first tried to share his pain about his wife's death, he ended up swallowing repeatedly and then sitting in silence for long periods of time. He could not speak for fear of releasing the anguish that was churning inside. As our visits continued, Sam became more comfortable talking about Irene and their fifty-year love affair. He was able to both laugh and cry while telling stories of their life together. It seemed that as Sam trusted the process of grief, he was able to move between the sadness of loss and the comfort of love with more confidence.

When the holiday season approached, though, Sam shook his head, with tears filling his eyes. The mountain of expected family traditions seemed insurmountable. When his eldest daughter wanted to host Thanksgiving and cook all of her mom's special dishes, Sam decided to bring Irene's well-loved stuffing bowl that had been passed around the Thanksgiving table for years. Sam explained that he had been afraid to try this idea. He was worried he would lose Irene all over again if he lost her belongings. But as he saw the bowl passed around the table, he realized that the love he shared with Irene could still be part of his life. In fact, it could give him life.

Sam followed his instincts and learned to continue loving Irene in a new way. He loved her not as someone only attached to the past or in his memories, but as someone who is a part of who he is now, in the present moment. He learned a love that is not limited to the common experience of possession. Instead, as Thomas Attig describes, Sam learned to love Irene with "the gentle embrace of partners in a dance. Rather than a way of *having* something, [our] loving becomes a way of *being with*."[8]

While some of us learn these lessons without the pain of death, Attig says that grief often teaches us that "our loving embrace of the dead in their absence is continuous with loving them when they are present. While our movements of loving exchange change after their death, they do not differ in kind. They can be dynamic and life-affirming."[9] These movements of love in our present moment teach us new steps for the dance and for our lives.

Something happens when we recognize love in the present moment. The veil is lifted, our hearts open, concerns fade away, and for the briefest of moments we encounter "the more." We have a glimpse into that which is greater than ourselves while at the same time being a part of us. Joy-filled moments easily reveal love's presence: a young couple sharing their proposal story, a new grandma describing the sleeping babe in her arms, a community's celebration of faith. We expect love and so are freed to say, "Yes, love is here."

How do we connect these times of joy with the uncertainty of our grief? How do we trust that when we let go we will actually be caught? Franciscan sister and professor Ilia Delio tells us, "[Saint] Bonaventure wrote that love is the gravity of the soul, it is what pulls us toward God. We could also say that love is the glue of the universe; it is what constantly holds everything together even when things fall apart."[10] With our eyes opened, we see love's presence in other moments of life: the neighbor who mowed our lawn, the firefighter who rescued a child, the friend who listened to our story. Love shines through the simple email that remembers a concern you shared two weeks ago. Love lives when you pick up your neighbor's mail. Each of these and more can and should be named as love in the present moment. Our hearts will vibrate with abundance and we will gain confidence in our capacity to see love in our grief.

Over several weeks of our bereavement work, Christine used colored pencils to sketch the hospital room where her daughter Kathy had died. Christine's heart mourned the cold, impersonal surroundings that defined Kathy's final days. Bravely, she reentered this unrelenting memory and drew a simple bed, a doorway, a square windowframe—the sterile hospital room that had denied Kathy's humanity. Christine told me again what had happened . . . cancer's dominance over a thirty-five-year-old body, the months of treatment and then decline, the helplessness that filled the hospital room. Over time, Christine added names to her drawing: the friends, family members, and caregivers who were present during the final days. Her stories revealed how each person brought light and love into the room. Slowly, as the names circled the hospital bed, Christine began to see that a circle of love and care had indeed surrounded Kathy, easing her way. Gradually, each name was decorated in color, the bed was covered with a warm blanket, and the sunlit window was decorated with curtains. Christine's surrender to her deepest grief allowed her to see and trust love's presence in the room and in her own heart. She reclaimed the memory of Kathy dying and carefully placed it into God's loving arms.

"Love is the gravity of the soul." Bonaventure's words bear repeating. They establish a clear orientation for our travels in the Land of Loss. We are created in love, called to live our lives with love, discover our best selves through love, and experience deep loss because of love. Love, in all its forms and definitions, is the force that attracts our soul and pulls it closer and closer to God. When we permit ourselves to see and name love in our grief, we find healing. Our heart is transformed.

As we discover love in the present moment, let us tune in to the simple miracles of life. Let us consider the reality of something greater than we are, that loves more than we can imagine. Let us open our hearts to receive love in the hidden places of who we are and who we hope to be. Love is the gravity of *your* soul, and is always calling you home.

Promptings of Hope

"Death ends a life, not a relationship." In *Tuesdays with Morrie*, sportswriter Mitch Albom wrote about the lessons he learned from his college professor's final months of life. Morrie Schwartz taught that the love created between people extends beyond death, touching hearts and transforming lives. Give yourself permission to experience love where you are in this moment and write a letter to your loved one.

You may want to catch him up on what has been happening in your life or who in the family is aggravating you. You might want to recount the things you miss about her and try to express your feelings about your loss. You can ask for guidance, say thank you, or share your deepest fears or dreams. Just pick up wherever you left off the last time you spoke with him or her and seek a reconnection through your letter. Let this be a sacred practice, for the connection you shared was one of love, and when you return to love you are not alone but part of the whole.

Create a private space, adding meaningful items if you wish—a lit candle, shells from the beach—and carve out a one- to two-hour period when you will not be disturbed. Be intentional with your choice of paper and pen.

Take some deep breaths, turning your attention to your body. Stretch your neck, shoulders, and the rest of your body, one section at a time. Let your concerns for the day slip away and allow your focus to soften. You are centering, bringing your awareness to the fullness of the created being you are.

Begin writing, *Dear* . . .

LOVE'S REMINDERS ALONG THE WAY

In *The Cure for Sorrow*, writer and ordained minister Jan Richardson offers blessings for those who are grieving. Page after page holds love-filled blessings to comfort the hurting hearts of those who feel broken, those who seek both solace and hope. She explains,

> A good blessing possesses something of what Celtic folk have long called a *thin place*, a space where the veil between worlds becomes permeable, and heaven and earth meet. . . . A thin place enables us to open our eyes and hearts to the presence of God that goes with us always. A blessing invites us to this same opening, that we might recognize and receive the help of the One who created us in love and encompasses us when we are at our most broken.[11]

Richardson's words inspire the understanding that blessings come into our life in many forms, through many openings. When blessings appear, they remind us that love is present in our grief and will sustain us as we heal.

Alan Wolfelt calls these blessings "wisdom teachings," and says that they are there to help us.[12] They are the reminders that love is still in our life, and love will guide us through this time of change. Grief is a mystery. Perhaps our best response is to surrender to that mystery and let love's blessings open our mind and touch our heart.

Four common experiences that reveal and nurture love's presence in our life are the lessons of nature, people who offer lovingkindness, times of challenge, and acts of compassion. As the author of the rest of your life, seek and receive these blessings around you.

THROUGH NATURE'S BEAUTY

Tia's mother died when she was a little girl. Now in her thirties, Tia sought a support group to honor and work with the feelings she had carried all these years. A group of women who had lost their parents was a good fit, and Tia bravely entered a conscious grieving process for her long-ago loss. During the session that focused on sources of support, each woman shared about the people, places, things, and thoughts that helped them in their grieving. Tia began telling a story about a recent experience she had in nature:

> I went for a walk in the woods near my house. I had been thinking about my mom the night before, and that morning walk felt like a prayer. I started noticing what was around me—the cool morning air against my skin, the light coming though the branches, the crunch my feet made on the ground. I felt so connected to this place just outside my kitchen window! I thought of my mom, who loved anything to do with nature, and felt connected to her too. When I saw a leaf moving with the wind, something moved within me. It was weird but I felt peace like I've never felt before.

As Tia told her story, the group saw her facial expressions change from curiosity to wonder to contentment. All sat quietly, and gratefully received this story of blessing.

Through the lens of the natural world, we learn to see loss differently. The tree that came down last winter has new growth at its base, a sign of hope. The lake bed previously drained of water is now covered with new plants and creatures that thrive in the sunlight. The change of seasons, year after year, echoes the back and forth of death and rebirth, endings and beginnings. Nature speaks, and if we listen, it will teach us of loss, grief, and renewal. When we are grounded in the rhythms of creation, we deepen our confidence that new life will follow death. In his book *Unattended Sorrow*, Stephen Levine reminds us that such blessings abound in "the design of the universe" and that "the whole of physics [is contained] in the swirls of a seashell; the constellations within a fleck of mica; the moon at the tip of a leaf in a droplet of water; the sun in a single falling snowflake; the evolution of a species in the high notes of a thrush."[13]

We can intentionally cultivate this perspective through the spiritual practice of sacred seeing, or *visio divina*. As we align ourselves with the natural world through sacred seeing, we open ourselves to moments of clarity and comfort. No longer separate and alone, we experience that which is bigger than ourselves and we open ourselves to listen and ponder. Poet and spiritual teacher Christine Valters Paintner explains it this way: "In visio divina, we move our awareness into our hearts and let our vision arise from this place of integration rather than analysis, and receptivity rather than grasping after the things we desire."[14]

THROUGH KIND AND LOVING PEOPLE

No doubt you have encountered wonderful, supportive people in your travels through the Land of Loss: the chaplain who sat with you in the hospital as you tried to comprehend what the doctor was saying; the nurses who cried as you said goodbye; your priest or pastor who listened quietly to your story. These and other professional caregivers have learned how to be supportive while respecting your boundaries. Each brought a little light into the dark days of loss.

Loving people are among us in many places and can be unexpected sources of support. Their warmth and empathy provide a resting place for our hurting hearts. As Alan Wolfelt instructs, "Spend time in the company of people who affirm your need to mourn yet at the same time give you hope for healing. People who are empathetic, nonjudgmental, good listeners, and who model positive, optimistic ways of being in the world will be your best grief companions."[15]

These supportive people are not there to "fix" us; in fact they may never hear the story of our loss. Those who freely offer loving energy have often faced their own losses and surrendered control over them. Their gentle presence or compassionate eyes kindle a knowing in our heart, a reminder of love. Their presence is a healing gift, their kindness a blessing.

Those with loving hearts may appear as the woman in the birdseed aisle, for example, or a new neighbor who drops off some farm-fresh eggs. They have no agenda except kindness. They are just being who *they* are, which gives you permission to figure out who *you* are. If you encounter such a person, take some extra time to get to know him or her. Relax, be yourself, and savor their kindness. The sense of humor, patience, or down-to-earth qualities that shine through them can be inspiring. As therapists Betsy Caprio and Thomas M. Hedberg make clear, "This person has learned to trust in the process of growth that is already underway, knowing that God is as much in charge of his or her unfolding as that of the acorn's or the rosebud's or the baby sparrow."[16] Listen for wisdom as you enjoy their presence. You might hear just the encouragement you need in that particular moment. Let their spark of life bring you comfort.

In *Praying Our Goodbyes*, Sister Joyce Rupp describes this evidence of love in our life as moments of kinship. In the Land of Loss, kinship is not limited to friendship or kinfolk; it is a rich bondedness that reaches out to us in our deepest places. Experiences of kinship include empathy and compassion, as well as a profound connection with another that supports our healing and transformation. As Sister Joyce clarifies:

> A union of spirits develops when one feels a value or a truth connected with the other who seems to walk some of the same inner footsteps of our own story of life. It's as if the vision in our own being meets the vision in another and something in us lights up in recognition, knowing that it is heard and accepted.[17]

In these moments, love has reached through the darkness and reminded us of the life beyond the pain, beyond the darkness. Surrounded by such love, we find courage to take one more step toward wholeness.

THROUGH TIMES OF CHALLENGE

There will be difficult reminders along the way. Love may be clothed in the unexpected—sometimes painful—encounter with your mother's best friend or your wife's work colleague. Or as life evolves and new spouses or children join the family, love sadly reminds you that your loved one is not here. Months or years may pass and you are suddenly thrust into the fresh ache of loss when you come upon a painting you both enjoyed. These moments are not evidence of your grief's regression. They are not cruel attacks to keep in you a state of longing. Instead, they are opportunities for healing an aspect of your heart that cries all alone.

Anne's father died when she was eleven. Her life changed as a result, but she found happiness and fulfillment in relationships and career. Anne married and raised a family, gratefully using her father's name for her first son. Years passed, her children grew up and started their own lives. One cold February, the date of March 1 kept returning to Anne's mind. She searched her memory but could not remember the significance of March 1, so she let the date become a part of her prayer. Anne trusted the arrival of this date to her thoughts and waited to learn its importance.

One morning, sitting at her desk at work, Anne was flooded with a depth of sadness that was inescapable . . . and she remembered. March 1, this very day, was her father's birthday. She let the tears fall, breathed through the pressure in her chest, and remembered the emptiness from his death so long ago. At the same time, Anne experienced a kindling of warmth and tenderness as she remembered love. She gave herself permission to experience this moment, even though it was attached to sadness. She did not dwell on forgetting her father's birthday, but chose to be grateful for this powerful reminder of love. As the waves of feeling passed through her, Anne stayed aware of the sweet love that touched her little-girl heart.

Emotional challenges along the way become reminders of love when we step in and become participants in the grieving process. Our accumulated wisdom has changed us, readying us to move into deeper layers of our feelings. While we do not welcome painful reminders of loss, we can learn to work with them. The lessons we have learned will help, as well as staying aware of love's presence in our daily life. With greater understanding, let us remember the invitation to keep an open heart, as John E. Welshons reminds us:

> Our hearts are our lifeline. If we react in fear and close them, we lose the healing potential and solace they offer.

> Our hearts have no boundaries—they are infinite. . . .
> True healing takes place when we open them to absorb
> our darkness, and swallow it into the infinite light they
> contain.[18]

Everything works together in the created being that we are
and moves us toward wholeness. Our call is to trust our capacity to heal and to rest in the promise of love. Our grief and all
its intricacies visit and revisit us throughout our lifetime. In
fact, the feelings of grief that arrive following our loved one's
death are not unknown feelings. We have held disappoint-
ments, losses, and grief all along. Stephen Levine says,

> It has been there all our lives, but it is only with the
> impact of unmistakable loss that we acknowledge it for
> the very first time. Perhaps if we recognized our ordi-
> nary grief sooner, we wouldn't be so overwhelmed by all
> that we have denied for so long.[19]

A retelling of an old Tibetan legend offers an image to help us
accept the painful, yet potentially healing, reminders that will
come: A woman sat alone one night, the fire glowing in the
single room. Three demons known as Doubt, Fear, and Guilt
decided to ambush her. They made a pact to dismantle her
home and that which she held dear. So they set about slamming cupboards and smashing dishes with confidence and
glee. But when they saw the woman tend to the fire and fill
the kettle, they became distracted and responded with louder
wails to get her attention. When she placed three cups on the
table, they stopped short and screamed, "What are you doing?
Why are you not afraid? We are here to take away your happiness!" The woman just looked at them, and shrugged her
shoulders as she put out the spoons, "I've met you all before

and I imagine you'll visit again. You might as well have a seat." Calmly, her eyes resting on each one, her voice without fear, she said, "What kind of tea would you like?"[20]

THROUGH ACTS OF COMPASSION

Compassion is best defined as "to suffer with." When we feel compassionate toward another, we open our hearts to their pain. We may experience compassion as kindness to others, or when our hearts are moved to sympathy or empathy. We might tap in to our tender places and pray that God's mercy would enfold another's pain. Our willingness to be present to suffering is an act of love, for when we choose love, we are not alone anymore but strengthened in our shared humanity. "Through the gate of compassion," Francis Weller writes, "we are invited to enter the wider conversation with all life. . . . It is through our experience with loss, sorrow, and pain that we deepen our connection with one another and enter the commons of the soul."[21]

If our loss was preceded by illness or painful decline, we may balk at the idea of reaching out to others in our time of bereavement. We may acknowledge that we are burnt out or emotionally tired. It is important to respect our own boundaries, especially during grief. We cannot easily measure the amount of energy we expend as we expend it, but we certainly know what it feels like when there is no more energy left! As it turns out, forcing ourselves to do good deeds can lead to further exhaustion and a misunderstanding of compassion.

However, when we are ready, our human capacity to feel, offer, and receive compassion is a valuable, life-giving resource. When we extend caring energy without expectation or condition, we enter an ever-present field of compassion. We discover a spacious, loving reality that lifts spirits and changes lives, our own included. Compassion for another becomes, somehow, a living moment within our own hearts. This loving exchange between souls creates space for Divine Love.

Cynthia Bourgeault's study of the beatitudes offers a window into the back and forth of compassion. "Exchange is the very nature of divine life—of consciousness itself, according to modern neurological science—and all things share in the divine life through participation in this dance of giving and receiving," she says.[22] Compassion is an active expression of love's flow between us, through us, and in us. We are wise to bring our hearts to such a space of healing and hope.

When Markus came to the bereavement support group, he admitted feeling cautious about sharing his feelings. He sat with the six other people in the room and introduced himself as task-oriented, the kind of person who relies on accomplishment for personal happiness. He described his frustration after his wife became ill. He could not "fix" her illness or her pain; he could not prevent her death. Markus felt helpless and, after her death, retreated to things he could manage at work or around the house.

Each person in the group shared their story of loss as they began an eight-week journey together. The process honored their differences and their common experience of loss. They learned how to listen without giving advice, judging, or placing expectations on each other. The weekly group became a sacred space for Markus and the other members as they held each other's hearts with tender mercy. They came to the group to help themselves, but in caring for each other they experienced the blessings of compassion.

Our conversation about compassion along the journey of grief must include the invitation to self-compassion. Just as a bereavement support group offers a safe space for grieving hearts, we would all benefit from such a space in the privacy of our home and the quiet of our mind. Moments of self-compassion, whether planned or spontaneous, reveal love's active presence in our hurting hearts. Simple, quiet reflection—laps in the pool or a slowly savored favorite meal—can become intentional and healing. While it would be easy for us to add self-compassion to the ever-lengthening to-do list for self-improvement that many of us carry, it is more empowering to see self-compassion as an act of love. It is an act that leads us to believe we are lovable. As Sister Doris Klein offers:

> We are the only ones who, with God, can truly hear our heart. Yes, we need outside witnesses and supportive others to companion us but, ultimately, we must sit with ourselves on this dark shore and acknowledge the truths around us. We must be the voice we hear in the night that says, "It's going to be okay. I will stay here with you. I will not abandon you. I will not go away."[23]

Self-compassion is challenging in our contemporary lives. There are already many demands on us and many who call for our help. At the same time, Francis Weller identifies self-compassion as "*the* root practice for our inner lives and also for our relational lives."[24] The stoicism, shame, or fractured sense of belonging that many of us carry will box us in and deny us the fullness of our inherent goodness. Loss turns everything around. Without our loved one's presence as a regular reminder of our worth, we must turn inward for love. Self-compassion teaches us to treat ourselves as we would treat a suffering child—with patience, kindness, and love. It is not easy, as Weller reminds us: "Every day we are asked to sit with pieces of our interior world that lie outside of what we find acceptable and welcome. . . . We have often treated these parts of ourselves with indifference, if not outright contempt."[25]

Perhaps our final surrender is stepping into the "immense Mystery of God that holds us in our solitary moments of distress,"[26] as Sister Doris Klein says, and believing we are loved and lovable. Death took the person who loved us, but grief returns us to the gift of compassionate love. When we choose compassion, for another and for ourselves, we step into the Mystery where we are one.

Promptings of Hope

"Grieving allows us to heal, to remember with love rather than pain. It is a sorting process. One by one you let go of things that are gone, and you mourn for them. One by one you take hold of the things that have become a part of who you are and build again." Rachel Naomi Remen's words in *Chicken Soup for the Grieving Soul* reflect the ongoing presence of love's reminders on your path. Each moment or experience that touches your heart is indeed part of who you are, shaping your present and nurturing your future. These blessings have come into your life as, perhaps, an unexpected email, sun shining through forest branches, a lost photograph now found, or a neighbor who needs your help. As Jan Richardson's "Solace Blessing" reminds us:

> *You do not even*
> *have to ask.*
>
> *Just leave it open—*
> *your door,*
> *your heart,*
> *your day*
> *in every aching moment*
> *it holds.*
>
> *See what solace*
> *spills through the gaps*

your sorrow has torn.

See what comfort
comes to visit,
holding out its gifts
in each compassionate hand.[27]

Create a "blessing bowl" to honor the gifts that have come your way:

1. Find the right bowl. It may be in your cupboard or at the local pottery shop. Choose one that warms your heart with hope. Place it in a special spot in your home.

2. Create a supply of small pieces of paper—cut-up index cards or strips of typing paper.

3. On a quiet day, think about your journey so far and identify moments when you felt warmed, affirmed, supported, loved. For each, write a word or symbol that captures that memory on one of the small pieces of paper. Place these notes, one at a time, into your blessing bowl. With each addition, give yourself time to give thanks for the gift of the moment that piece of paper represents.

As life goes forward, "see what comfort comes to visit." Keep your eyes open for love's entry into your heart. Add these new blessings as they appear, always with gratitude for their arrival and with hope for your healing.

PART 4

Changed

Some travelers say they can feel the waters from the
Fountain of Hope all throughout the Land of Loss.
Its droplets are far-reaching, healing each step on the
journey. Some talk about the fountain with hushed
voices, as they walk toward its surging waters of life and
love. They are more than ready to be showered with life-
giving hope. The fountain's ancient springs lie beneath
the Land of Loss as a quiet but constant presence for all
and a secret passageway to the Land of Hope.

While our entry into Changed may feel tentative at times, once we step into this region of the Land of Loss, we are indeed transformed. We are on our way to accepting a "new normal." For some of us, hope has taken root, and we can see new possibilities of life before us. Grief has challenged our assumptions, stimulated our potential, and demanded that we reconsider what our life can be. With grief's help, we hear Sister Joyce Rupp's reminder, "There is a new country waiting for us. There are new melodies that yearn to be sung in our spirits. We must believe this even on our most desolate of days. The season of springtime, of hello, awaits us all."[1]

In Changed, we see a path that contains all we have learned, especially the lessons of love. Loss set change in motion, but love shapes our transformation. We have felt the anguish of loss and know the cost of love. We know the pain that loss exacts on tender hearts. If we have found our way to Changed, though, we also know that it was worth it. It will always be "worth it" to love another, to love God, and even to love ourselves. In doing so, we join our hearts with that which makes us whole. Love has made room for loss. We do not have to choose one over the other. Love expands in our evolving heart and we continue to explore our deepening relationship with ourselves. Grief has turned our attention to our tenderness, our needs, our desires. Loss has led us to a new imperative: that which we love will flourish, so let us learn to love, deeply and confidently.

As we find our footing, we begin with the practice of gratitude. A grateful heart guides us through our feelings and grounds us in the gift of our relationship. We return to J. William Worden's tasks—the fourth and final task is to find an enduring connection with your loved one while embarking on a new life. Our new horizon leads us into creative ritual as well, to nurture that connection and our unique needs. The isolation we felt upon entering the Land of Loss has changed, replaced perhaps by a sense of wholeness, a call to compassion, or a hard-won maturity. Alan Wolfelt reminds us, "When you leave the wilderness of your grief, you are simply not the same person as you were when you entered the wilderness. You have been through so much. How could you be the same?"[2]

CHAPTER 9

CONTEMPLATE A NEW HORIZON

At this point on our journey with grief, our life may feel experimental, as we "try on" new understandings of ourselves, others, and the mystery that surrounds us. This type of change moves subtly into our lives with opportunities to respond in new ways or add new priorities. When we step into and help shape the life before us, we shed attitudes—sometimes for just an hour at a time—that restrict our vision of the future. In *Praying Our Goodbyes*, Sister Joyce Rupp puts it this way:

> We choose to use our energies in another way, giving them another direction. Instead of concentrating on what has been hurtful, we look to what will be life-giving. We wish that life could be otherwise or that things could be different. But it cannot be so, so we accept that fact and move forward. We continue to care deeply but we also realize that we cannot change what is.[1]

As we contemplate the new horizon before us, we are creating a new relationship with ourselves. This is an important step in our journey through grief. It lays the groundwork for our transition into the Land of Hope. This personal growth can be overlooked in our drive to retain the past, with our focus being on our loved one and the "lost" relationship. But every up and down or twist and turn along the path brings us face-to-face with ourselves. Every experiment with our grief, spiritual practice, or commitment to self-care leads us to a deeper understanding of who we are. With this awareness, we may be willing to see ourselves as our loved ones did—as brave, thoughtful, and worthy of love.

Grief, our ally and companion, reminds us of a central truth that is hidden within our tears and fears: The one whom we grieve loved us. We are lovable. When we accept this truth, we are free to build on that foundation and learn to love ourselves in new ways. We learn to move beyond the self-conscious model of self-love. Instead, we enter the mystery of soul. In *The Wild Edge of Sorrow*, Francis Weller writes, "To hold our grief in front of us and tend it with time, patience, and compassion is an act of great devotion—it is an act of the heart. In the long run, change is as much devotional as it is psychological. It is out of love that we ultimately reshape our lives."[2]

Look out over this new horizon and create a space of regard for the steps ahead. To begin, turn to gratitude and ritual to support your soul work. Each is integral to the development of an interior life and each continues the conversation with our grief. Gratitude adds a gentle layer to our transformed relationship with our loved one. By receiving the gift that he or she was in our life, we open our heart to other sources of love. Ritual can play a significant role in our soul's journey with grief as well. Rituals keep us in the present moment, where memories and dreams rest together, without expectation but with an attitude of reverence. The horizon before us is new but at the same time it can feel like we are coming home.

A GRATEFUL HEART

Grieving with a grateful heart creates balance in our grief. Our memories evolve into comforting reminders of our loved one. Certain moments come to mind; we celebrate them; and in doing so, we honor the life of this one person. Gratitude gives a focus beyond loss and allows us to experience new feelings and consider other outlooks. For some, Alan Wolfelt explains, gratitude is a reminder that "you have to live not only for yourself but for the precious person in your life who has died—to work on their unfinished work and to realize their unfinished dreams."[3]

Robert A. Emmons, a leading scientific expert on gratitude, defines gratitude as "the knowing awareness that we are the recipients of goodness."[4] With gratitude's assistance we see the blessing of that goodness in our lives. Our memories become generative sources of hope and love, as gratitude offers a rich alternative to the more painful sides of grief and becomes a passageway into a deeper sense of spirit.

When we cultivate gratitude in the privacy of our hearts, we expand our capacity to love. Brother David Steindl-Rast, in *Gratefulness, the Heart of Prayer*, explains that the growth process in gratefulness begins with awareness. "We must recognize the gift as gift, and only our intellect can do that,"[5] Brother David says. In the Land of Loss, too, we begin with the recognition that our loved one has been a gift in our life. We can realize the blessing we have received through this one unique relationship, even with sadness in our hearts.

The next step in growing gratitude is acknowledgment. Brother David explains that acknowledging a gift is difficult for some of us, because in doing so we must also acknowledge a kind of dependence on the giver. For example, some people squirm uncomfortably when offered a compliment. Others may feel embarrassed when receiving a gift if they have none in return.

The simple idea of *receiving* can trigger discomfort because many of us link acknowledgment with obligation. According to Brother David, "When I acknowledge a gift received, I acknowledge a bond that binds me to the giver. But we tend to fear the obligations this bond entails. . . . We want to be self-sufficient."[6]

Consequently, the step of acknowledgment is sometimes delayed in our development of gratitude. We hold to the normal human desire for self-sufficiency—consider how toddlers push away to walk on their own, or how our aging parents keep their car keys as long as they can. We try to convince ourselves that we can be "strong." But at the same time, grief has helped us, almost forced us, to accept our vulnerability. We have encountered and perhaps valued the tender side of ourselves that appears in grief. This, then, becomes our access point to acknowledge the gift given. If we have learned to open our heart, we will be able to receive with open hands. This is the stance of gratitude that we seek.

The final step in our soul's journey toward gratefulness, as outlined by Brother David, is recognizing our *inter*dependence, our mutual reliance on one another. As Brother David describes,

> The interdependence of gratefulness is truly mutual. The receiver of the gift depends on the giver. . . . When we give thanks, we give something greater than the gift we received, whatever it was. The greatest gift one can give is thanksgiving. . . . In giving thanks, we give ourselves.[7]

Brother David invites us to see the sacred exchange that gratitude creates. Our loved one's presence in our lives was and is a gift. With acknowledgment, we can gratefully receive all that gift entails—love, approval, patience. Our "thank-you" becomes a gift in return. With thanksgiving, our soul participates in an exchange that transcends loss and strengthens the bond between ourselves and our loved one.

The beats of a grateful heart draw us through the emptiness of absence to the calm of presence. Gratitude teaches us to bring more of ourselves to each day. When we live with greater fullness, we might hear ourselves say, "My life has room for me" or "There is something good in *this* day." We sense our own presence peeking out as we return to laughter. We come back to ourselves with memories of riding a new bike or running in the rain. Sometimes we experience our deceased loved one's presence; we are touched by a feeling of deep connection, and our transformed relationship seems life-giving. Some of us may be gifted with an experience of Divine Presence where our soul rests in a space of reverence and awe.

When we practice gratitude, love's healing energy flows through us and toward others, often rekindling our human connection with Mystery. This is the stuff of new life and active hope. Though our hearts may still ache from loss or become wary of the unknown all around us, we come to understand that the depth of our grief is often a counterpoint to the love shared with another. We certainly know that no one else can love us in exactly the same way that he or she did. The experience of that one relationship, with all its complexities, is a gift. Our soul's best response to this gift? A deep and heartfelt "thank-you."

Promptings of Hope

"I still miss those I loved who are no longer with me but I find I am grateful for having loved them. The gratitude has finally conquered the loss," writes novelist Rita Mae Brown in *Starting from Scratch*.

Each step you take to build gratitude into your life will create space for healing in your heart. Begin with "thank-you." In the quiet of the morning, when your mind turns to what is missing, consider what is present and say "thank-you." Breathe "thank-you" for the fresh air, or sing "thank-you" for this new day. Spend time with memories, and offer a "thank-you" to childhood neighbors, your favorite pet, or a past success. When you are ready, whisper "thank-you" for the one who loved you.

When such seeds of gratitude are planted, memories become not just a reminder of loss but also a source of life. Every "thank-you" allows your soul to sing the song of love it carries deep within.

RITUAL FOR THE SOUL

When Yvonne lost her sister, Karyn, it was as if a part of herself had died. They had been close all their lives, and Yvonne could not imagine a world without Karyn in it. Karyn's death was a long, hospital-driven ordeal in another state. Yvonne's emotions were pulled back and forth between Karyn's bedside and the home she shared with her young daughter and husband. In the end, Yvonne prayed for her sister to find relief from pain and suffering in a peaceful death. Her own heart, though, was broken.

As everything settled, Yvonne entered the emptiness of her grief. She loved her life with her husband and daughter but felt trapped in the pain of her loss. Yvonne and her husband had talked about another baby but that idea now seemed far away. In her deepest place, Yvonne knew the best way to heal from her loss was to find a way to bring Karyn into her life, where she had always been. One night Yvonne started telling childhood stories to her daughter and, in doing so, recaptured some of the joy she had felt as a little girl. She described sweet memories of her sister as they laughed through adventures of apple picking and firefly catching. Her voice quieted as she remembered their sacred promises of secrecy under the covers in their bedroom. The nighttime stories between Yvonne and her daughter became a ritual that included a special dragonfly night-light. Buying it seemed like a simple choice, but as her little girl's bedtime routine evolved, Yvonne realized something had changed. She had changed. The dragonfly's glow filled the room and her heart. Karyn was no longer a memory to be captured but rather a tangible part of their lives.

Rituals keep us grounded in the present moment. Sometimes they evolve without expectation, sometimes with an attitude of reverence. Yvonne trusted her instincts as her heart guided the creation of a family ritual. By listening to her own needs and responding to them with love, Yvonne's ritual touched the sacred, as rituals often do. In *To Dance with God*, author and educator Gertrud Mueller Nelson explains ritual in this way:

> The making of ritual is a creative act fundamental in human life. . . . What is too vast and shapeless, we deal with in small, manageable pieces. We do this for practicality but we also do this for a higher purpose: to relate safely to the mysterious, to communicate with the transcendent.[8]

As grievers, we may not be actively seeking a spiritual experience. Yet our grief leads us to the space of reverence where we meet our soul. As it turns out, ritual speaks the language of soul because of its ability to both embrace and transcend the realities of human life.

EMBRACING PERSONAL RITUAL

We often depend upon professional, institutional, or religious leaders to provide opportunities for ritual, and their support is critical in the early pain of loss. The prescribed wakes, funerals, memorial services, and burials offer comfort and community. As we have learned, these public gatherings enfranchise grief. They offer structure for the expression of feelings and opportunities for meaning-making during a time of confusion. Research has shown, however, that the changes in contemporary life have led to a decrease in formal ritual traditions. In the United States, for example, many people are more mobile and experience a "lack of belonging" in communities. The result, according to researcher and professor Robert Neimeyer, is the "deritualization of death and bereavement" that creates a form of disenfranchisement. As Neimeyer explains, "One clear trend is that traditional rites and rituals for structuring major life transitions of all kinds have declined in authority in much of the world, though the need for helping people acknowledge, understand, and negotiate such events remains as compelling as ever."[9]

This cultural shift leaves "those [who are] bereaved by a death [with] no idea what to do next," writes Therese Rando.[10] When traditional public forms of ritual are not available or their timing is inadequate, we can turn to personal bereavement rituals to transform loss into legacy. Rando continues,

> Rituals can provide a structured way for you to recall your lost loved one and to make some statement about your feelings. Since they acknowledge the physical loss of your loved one while allowing memory to continue, they can serve to encourage your necessary formation of a new relationship with the deceased.[11]

Ritual wakes up the wisdom within us, reconnecting us with Mystery. Francis Weller explains, "Ritual is a direct form of knowing, something indigenous to the psyche. It has evolved with us, taking knowing into the bone, into our very marrow. I call ritual *embodied process*."[12]

Yvonne's experience with ritual, for example, evolved organically. Each step led to the next. She did not set out to have a "special moment"; she did not place expectations upon their bedtime stories. Instead, she trusted her own sense of what she needed. We can learn from Yvonne as we develop our own awareness of where grief is calling us. Our response becomes our participation with our grief, what I have been calling "conscious grieving." Our actions—thinking about, or planning, or implementing a gesture of remembrance— become an embodiment of our heart's song of grief.

In *The Other Side of Sadness*, George Bonanno tells a personal story of his participation in the Chinese bereavement ritual of burning "joss" paper in a temple. After describing the cultural history of this foreign ritual and his personal struggle with claiming his father's memory within a strained relationship, he shared an epiphany. The act of standing before the furnace, with specially selected paper in hand, heightened his feelings of connection to his dad. "Immediately I began to feel my father's presence," Bonanno writes, "much as I had when I had occasionally spoken to him in the past, but this was like opening a door to another world."[13] As he stayed with this awareness, waiting his turn at the furnace, he opened his heart to other thoughts and feelings about his father and discovered a brand-new connection. This trip to China represented the travel his father was unable to make in his life; the sacrifice he gave to support his family. Suddenly the researcher let go, became his father's son, and felt that the "disparate strands of our relationship seemed to knit together for the first time. It seemed to wrap itself around me. I felt indelibly linked with my father. He was me and I was him."[14]

All the elements of this highly stylized ritual enabled this moment of awareness. With reflection, Bonanno understood that the ritual had created a space where he was open to new thoughts and feelings, to psychic shifts, to whispers from the Divine. He said yes to the Mystery. "And then I realized that *thinking* about my father this way was the whole point. . . . The actual burning of the offerings was an afterthought, literally: the most vital part of the ceremony had already happened."[15]

CREATING RITUAL

Our loss creates unique opportunities for ritual. When the public events are over or when certain circumstances trigger our feelings and memories, ritual provides a structure that holds our grief, that gives it meaning and space for healing and transformation. Therese Rando tells us,

> Your ritual need not be overly dramatic to be useful. It only has to be tailored to your individual needs and pertain to the specific loss you have experienced. If it is, and it assists you in your grief work, then by definition it will be meaningful and therapeutic for you.[16]

A walk on the beach, selling the truck, a moment of silence—each may be a mundane act within your day. When done with intention and awareness, however, your experience is deepened. Each act becomes a connection with your loved one, a part of the soul language that leads you forward into a life-giving space. The walk on the beach, for example, becomes more than exercise; it evolves into a time of sacred communion with your loved one or with God. "Planting a garden and tending to the chemistry of your compost pile can become a therapy that lets you know in your very bones that life's [challenges] can be transformed into a blooming and rich new growth," offers Gertrud Mueller Nelson.[17] With intention, our choices become our prayer as we trust the unspoken truth that lives within our daily life.

The following settings for ritual, and many of the "Promptings of Hope" and other suggestions in this book, provide examples of the range that ritual covers. Our personal rituals are not dependent upon a prescribed format; rather, they are born out of our story. They move us into a deeper relationship with that which is greater than our story. Ritual, Francis Weller writes, "sutures the tears in the soul that occur in the daily rounds of living" and provides "the container, the safe space generated within the ritual field, [that] is capable of holding the intensity of emotions associated with these aspects of soul."[18]

The time we give to planning a ritual becomes sacred time, as we open our heart to the unknown. After completing a ritual, our soul moves toward a place of deep healing. We experience the present moment with eyes wide open to the life within and around us. The symbols and gestures establish and strengthen a sacred connection to our loved one.

RITUAL FOR LIFE EVENTS

Our loved one's absence seems to leap out when we face a family wedding or the annual reunion. Experiences such as the holiday season, the anniversary of his death, or her birthday can trigger strong feelings of loss, even after some time has passed. Personal ritual provides a pause that honors our grief and our loved one's memory as we prepare to share time with family and friends. Therese Rando calls this a "delimitation of grief," or setting a boundary around our feelings.

Ritual can channel your feelings into an activity having a distinct beginning and ending with a clear purpose. In this way, it can make your feelings more manageable, especially during holidays and other anniversary times.[19]

Marilyn's husband, Joe, died two years before their daughter, Susan, got engaged. During the wedding planning, Susan created a ritual that included her three stepbrothers from her dad's previous marriage. Since they had always been part of her life, they were happy to share in the memory of their father on their little sister's wedding day. After the ceremony, at the traditional time of the father-daughter wedding dance, each brother took a turn and danced with Susan to the Beatles' tune "In My Life." Everyone at the wedding watched with tears in their eyes, knowing that Joe was present as Susan was held so lovingly. Marilyn, Susan, and her brothers were free to enter the celebration, as Joe and their grief were honored in ritual.

RITUAL FOR PAST LOSSES

While we move back into life following loss, we never truly forget our loved one. Their memory returns on certain occasions or as our life takes a turn. We may realize that we miss their counsel. Our loved one is a part of us, and sometimes we return to sadness. The best response is to trust the call back into loss and to trust our feelings. Remember, healing is not a linear experience; other losses or unfinished grief may pull us into painful places. This is not evidence of unsuccessful grieving. It is confirmation that we are human, that life influences us, that we love. Fortunately, rituals can reach back through time to offer light and healing from a new vantage point. They might renew the sadness, but they also renew the love shared and encourage further healing. As Rando explains, "Rituals give you permission to outwardly express your feelings. They provide acceptable outlets for your feelings and give you symbols to focus on."[20]

At eighty, Rosalie sought support for her husband's and son's recent deaths. In the process of working with her experience of loss, she began talking about the two little babies she had miscarried so many years ago. She bravely decided to step into her feelings and write a letter to the infants, along with letters to her son and husband. She gave careful attention to special stationery and a container to hold the completed letters. Rosalie's ritual acknowledged her return to the Land of Loss and honored the places in her heart that remembered and loved her babies. Her years had given her the courage and wisdom to open her heart to their memory.

RITUAL AND LEGACY

"Participation in rituals gives you the chance to interact intensely with the memory of your deceased loved one for a limited period of time in a healthy fashion,"[21] Rando says. Much like the Dual Process Model's explanation of grief that we discussed earlier, ritual gives us permission to move into sad or other feelings, knowing that we will move out of them as well. This example of oscillation frees us to explore and express feelings, especially regarding the legacy of our loved one. Planting a new garden, for example, creates an opportunity to connect with our loved one's passion for life. Every choice in the process has meaning and will support our healing. The type of flowers, decorative stones, trellises, or ornamental grasses—each element bounces between our heart and our memories to communicate the gift of our loved one's life. This type of ritual establishes a life-giving connection while respecting our need to engage with their memory.

Cora's husband died after they had been married fifty-one years. Their children and grandchildren shared in her grief for this vibrant, loving man. Cora told many stories of his generosity and humor. As she processed her loss, Cora looked at

the dresser drawers full of T-shirts that her husband had col-
lected over the years. Each T-shirt told a story of an adventure
that he and Cora had shared with their family. Cora decided
to cut, sew, and fill T-shirts to turn them into pillows, and
share them with family and friends. Her husband's spirit was
brought to life in this ritual of remembering. Cora's heart was
warmed by her creative expression and by the joy of sharing
the transformed T-shirts.

RITUAL AND CELEBRATION

As we think about the places where ritual makes sense in
our own grief, it is helpful to recall the many moments that
ritual has already played a role in our story. Past celebrations
naturally included key elements: a special outfit for a birthday
party, a gift for a housewarming, a favorite song or story at a
retirement party, and food, always food, to offer sustenance.
Celebrations may have included balloons, poignant remarks,
and blessings. Any and all of these can be woven into a personal ritual to highlight the gift of life that we found with our
loved one and to celebrate their presence in our life.

Maureen and her sister, Barbara, shared a lifetime of
memories and loving support of one another. Two months
after Barbara's death, Maureen made a painful change in her
work life. This transition in ministry—Maureen is a religious
sister—complicated and delayed her grief, causing a heavy
weight in her heart for the next few years. While on a sabbati-
cal, Sister Maureen chose to enter her Land of Loss through
a retreat on loss and grief. She found the space to express her
feelings, and something shifted inside. She explains, "I know
that I experienced a great freedom in unleashing that burden
of grief but I also think, at least for me, ritual is very important." Sister Maureen made a plan to celebrate Barbara's next
birthday, which also happened to be St. Patrick's Day. She

wore green and enjoyed dinner at an Irish restaurant with a friend. "That evening, in the solitude of my room, I had bought a small rose plant, my sister's favorite flower, played some music, gave thanks for her life and the blessing of the time to remember, celebrate, and believe that all is well."

RITUAL AND OTHERS

Our discussion so far has been on the benefits of personal ritual at various points in the journey. Sometimes it is meaningful to include others in a personal ritual, because their witness adds dimension and energy to the experience. Collective ritual legitimizes the outward expression of feelings, and, as Rando explains, it "cuts through intellectualization and other resistances to mourning to directly reach your emotions."[22]

Shared ritual also enables social connection around the loss, providing a comforting place for our feelings. The addition of others in personal ritual requires more planning, but the experience can bring new life and love to the time of remembering.

Nancy invited two good friends to the cemetery to remember her mother, Marge. She explained to them that her mom loved standing in the wind; she said it felt as if life were wrapping itself around her. Marge also used to make jokes about the wind's music making as it blew through the holes of her metal crutches. Nancy and her friends stood together at the cemetery, waving pinwheels in the wind. In this space of joy-filled remembering, Nancy allowed her tears to fall. Her personal but shared ritual created an intimate moment that acknowledged multiple feelings. Her friends, loving witnesses to her healing process, helped Nancy celebrate her mother's love of life.

SPONTANEOUS RITUAL

Opportunities to remember and ritualize events occur throughout your life. The moment appears and your loved one enters your heart. You might come across an old birthday card from her and take time to read its handwritten message. With tears and a smile, you offer a silent thank-you and put the card on the mantel for a few days . . . just because. A hike or kayak trip might bring you to a spot in nature that he would have loved . . . you stop, remember, touch a tree or the water as your heart touches love. These unexpected rituals are your soul's opportunity to enter into the conversation of remembering and healing. Chaplain and minister Alice Parsons Zulli shares:

> Ritual is sacred. Rituals can restore a sense of balance to life. Although many of us create ceremonies or rituals for one occasion or another, few understand why rituals help in adjusting to change. Even fewer understand the power of ritual to strengthen the bonds that connect us. . . . Death and grief are experiences that may make us feel helpless or out of control as emotional and physical energy is thrown out of balance. Rituals or ceremonies link physical and mental expression in a way that allows us to express and act out feelings and beliefs.[23]

Promptings of Hope

"Each of us has cause to think with deep gratitude of those who have lighted the flame within us." Albert Schweitzer reminds us of the enduring presence of our loved ones in our lives today. Look for and experiment with very small actions of remembering. If the examples below resonate, try them! These gentle but visible expressions of love are rituals in their simplest form. At the same time, keep your eyes open for opportunities for ritual that come out of your own life and story.

- Place a ribbon of remembrance on the birdfeeder you two enjoyed.

- Drive to your favorite restaurant, sit outside, and thank your loved one for sweet memories.

- Create simple Christmas ornaments in his memory and share them with family and friends.

- Buy yourself a gift that she might have given you, and enjoy it.

- Light a candle and remember.

- Add or change a holiday decoration that honors his absence.

- At a gathering of friends or family, place small gifts at the table settings to remember her together.

- Play your game of tennis or golf with a memento of your loved one tucked into your gear, cheering you on.

CHAPTER 10

LAND OF HOPE

What will our individual Land of Hope look like? We don't know. We may see glimpses, we may actively participate in shaping its terrain, but there is always an element of mystery. Our task in Changed, along with cultivating enduring relationships with ourselves and our loved one, is to befriend Mystery, in its fullness, and to trust the path before us. "The unfolding of a new life may take us through unexpected territory. . . . Even when we don't know what lies ahead, we can learn daily from an increasing warmth to trust the process," Stephen Levine reminds us in *Unattended Sorrow*.[1] Every step we've taken has brought us to this point. Every lesson, tear, and memory have contributed to our capacity to imagine the possibility of life with hope in it. As the meaning-makers of our own lives, we gather our resources and shape a life that is in alignment with our loving heart. We relearn the relationship with our loved one and trust the gift of that connection. We move out into hope—perhaps tentatively at first—with a renewed capacity for love.

Hope is so much more than wishful thinking. As seasoned travelers in the landscape of loss, we move past childish images of hope. We know it's more than Merriam-Webster's definition: "to want something to happen or be true." Our experiences have taught us that desires skim the surface in our understanding of hope. And yet we want hope in our lives. We look deep within, asking "What does hope look like for me? How does it feel in my body and in my life?" A, supposedly, archaic definition of hope offers us a more grounded meaning: "the assured reliance on the character, ability, strength, or truth of someone or something." This image of hope moves us away from expectation toward a place of confidence.

Hope lives in the present. With an underpinning of surrender, hope is a resting place for our weary soul. At the same time, hope transcends the present. Hope leads us, with an "orientation of the spirit," toward a life filled with joy and love. Playwright and former Czechoslovakian president Václav Havel writes,

> Hope . . . is a dimension of the soul, and is not essentially dependent on some particular observation of the world. . . . It is an orientation of the spirit, an orientation of the heart; it transcends the world that is immediately experienced, and is anchored somewhere beyond its horizons.[2]

Reweaving Our Connection

While human beings have a long history of memorializing loved ones to sustain a connection with them, we sometimes wonder if there is something wrong or unhealthy about ongoing relationships with the deceased. Religious traditions offer prescribed masses for the dead or a yearly lighting of the Yahrzeit candle, but without (or because of) the formality and guidance of religious leaders we might doubt our instincts to sustain emotional or spiritual connections. Contemporary researchers have studied human response to loss around the world. They have found that practices to maintain active relationships with deceased loved ones, such as in Japan and Mexico, portray grief as a process of adaptation that respects our natural human rhythms. So why do we in Western culture particularly experience hesitation or self-consciousness when we think about an ongoing relationship with deceased loved ones? Interestingly, "only in the past one hundred years have continued bonds been denied as a normal part of bereavement behavior," explain researchers Phyllis R. Silverman and Dennis Klass.[3] One reason is Sigmund Freud's 1917 understanding of grief. Unfortunately, his belief that the goal of grief is "disengagement from the loved one" birthed years of influence that has filtered down to the current common prescription to "move on." Freud's dominant model of grief coincided with the arrival of twentieth-century cultural modernism, where the social focus became "goal directedness, efficiency, and rationality. . . . When applied to grief, this view suggests that people need to recover from their intense state of emotionality and return to normal functioning and effectiveness as quickly and efficiently as possible."[4] Our current attitude toward grief is influenced by these two strands of thought. But we have learned that the drive to "move on" in an efficient manner minimizes the grieving process, as well as the bonds created by loving relationships. As George Bonanno points out, compelling research shows that "healthy, bereaved people did not relinquish the emotional bond. In fact, many continued to feel deeply connected."[5]

J. William Worden, who provided this book's theoretical touchstones, had his own evolution on the topic of continuing bonds. His work reflects our culture's changing outlook toward these ongoing relationships and gives further recognition of their role in grief. In the first edition of his *Grief Counseling and Grief Therapy* (1982), Worden presented the fourth task of mourning as "withdrawing emotional energy from the deceased and reinvesting it in another relationship." His teaching reflected the dominant thinking of the time: successful grief is a "decathexis," or a retracting of one's emotional investment. Nine years later, the second edition redefined the task: "to emotionally relocate the deceased and move on with life." This language remained through the third (2001) edition and affirmed the value of emotional connections with deceased loved ones. The fourth edition of *Grief Counseling and Grief Therapy* was published in 2009, and the fourth task was rewritten once again: "to find an enduring connection with the deceased in the midst of embarking on a new life." This is our mantra in Changed. Task four, aligned with current bereavement theory, invites a space for our loved ones to remain in our hearts, while nurturing our desires "to go on living effectively in the world."[6] Contemporary bereavement theorists still study and explain the value of continuing bonds, or braids of love, as we call them in the Land of Hope. George Bonanno describes this return to the continuation, not elimination, of emotional bonds as a sea change in our understanding of grief.

There are some factors that should be mentioned, however, for a full understanding of these bonds' place in our healing. Continuing bonds are not an alternative to grief-work, but more a result of it. The emotional swings and unexpected vulnerability at the outset of grief deserve our full attention, our conscious participation. Bonanno explains that as we move "toward emotional equilibrium, it becomes easier to utilize these kinds of bonding experiences to sustain a sense of calm and connection."[7]

Grief has helped us be honest about our expectations and needs; our travels have helped us grow from the inside out. But our human nature is complex. Thomas Attig warns that if we get caught in a static or dependent relationship with the memory of our loved one, for example, we may "compromise, undermine, or stifle the full development of our personal subjectivity and individuality."[8] Alternatively, some of us may become preoccupied by unfinished business in the continuing relationship. We may be unable to lift the "barrier of our sorrow," as C. S. Lewis describes it, unable to experience the joys and richness of love that lie ahead, because our focus is on the past. Dependency and unfinished business represent the type of grief-work that we may need to address, even in this later phase of our journey, if we are to cultivate life-giving braids of love. We've likely sustained wounds through our loss and believe that we've managed them. Dependency and unfinished business are two reminders that there is more healing to do, and these very real nuances to our story deserve their own focus and loving attention.

Continuing bonds do not erase the pain of loss. Instead, they keep love alive as we continue to heal. It is important to trust our unique process, to respect its call. Attig clarifies:

> No two of us relearn our relationship with the deceased by meeting identical challenges. Reintegration of our relationships within our present living, in understanding our individual biographies, and in our patterns of self-transcending connection, demands different things for each of us. Each of us takes a distinctive course, and, as we do, the deceased finds a distinctive place in each of our lives as our losses and grieving transform them.[9]

The braids of love invite us into a sacred connection that honors our attachment to our loved one while accepting the reality of the separation. This is a delicate dance, one we might not have learned when our loved one was alive. Our relationships can create attachments that obscure the fact that our loved one is a separate individual, with his or her own fears, goals, and perceptions. Following death, though, the braids of love recognize our attachment *within the context of* separation. We are connected, and yet we are not; we are one, and yet we are two. This was true while our loved one was alive, and it is true now. "As we learn to love in this way, we learn to let go and let be," Attig explains:

> Some of us learned these lessons prior to [the] death. . . . Some of us learn them only after our loved one's death, when the reality of not having the one we love comes crashing in. The deeper truth is that we never had the person as a possession even when he or she was alive.[10]

When death took our loved one away, it might have felt like our connection, our braid of love, was severed. But the braid of love does not cease to be; it is made of stronger stuff than a human body. We have the capacity to reweave and tend to these braids. As we journey deeper and deeper into who we are, we recover parts of ourselves that might have been absent for a while. With courage, we retrieve lost strands and weave them back into the braid, reanimating ourselves and the connection. Treasured memories enrich and enliven the braids, and we are renewed. They hold the blessing of our loved one's presence in our lives. Our tears may still fall, but they fall upon the torn places, healing them and restoring love's bond. As a ritual spoken in the Jewish tradition reminds us,

> Memory can tell us only what we were, in company with those we loved; it cannot help us find what each of us, alone, must now become. Yet no person is really alone; those who live no more echo still within our thoughts and words, and what they did has become woven into what we are.[11]

The braid of love we created with our loved one transcends death and becomes a reliable and creative resource for life. As it turns out, our loved one, once again, continues to support our growth and well-being. Through love, we exchange life-giving energy that sustains our soul in the land before us.

Promptings of Hope

"In the tapestry of life, we're all connected. Each one of us is a gift to those around us, helping each other be who we are." Author Anita Moorjani reminds us in *Dying to Be Me* that our loved one is part of who we are today. Our connection extends across death's chasm right into our hearts in the present moment. With this awareness, we are empowered to enter wisdom's teachings in the moment before us. Unencumbered by the past's longings or the future's fears, the present moment is a deep well of wonder and hope.

Mandalas offer a sacred process to encounter the present moment. The simple invitation to fill a circle provides a pathway into ourselves that can be calming, enlightening, and healing. The following exercise, taken from *Honoring the Soul: Mandalas for Inspiration and Insight*, by Rose Amodeo Petronella, guides us into a contemplative practice that connects us to our deepest self.

- Get comfortable, with materials in front of you: a piece of paper with a circle on it, and a pen, colored pencils, markers, crayons, clay, or collage materials.

- Close your eyes and relax every part of your body, as much as possible, setting aside whatever is on your mind for the time being. Take a few deep breaths and sit quietly until you feel your body relax. You may want to sit in silence or listen to soft music.

- Ask yourself, "How am I feeling?" (For example: happy, hurt, excited, worried, sad, scared, mad, confused, grateful, etc.) Journaling may help you identify what is going on inside you.

- Receive whatever comes to you and let it be. Try not to judge it, but just let it be.

- When you are ready, let a color or collage item choose you (so to speak), and begin creating your mandala. Try not to think about it too much, but just let it happen. There is no right or wrong way to do this.

- Accept whatever comes. This is your mandala, and your style is unique to you at this moment in time. The way it is, is the way it's supposed to be for now. If you feel so moved, imagine the Divine is sitting with you an gazing at your creation with you. Is there something you want to say to the Divine? If so, speak from your heart and listen for a response. If it seems right, write some or all of this communication on or around your mandala.

- When it feels complete, sign it and write the date and the feeling.

- Appreciate it. Look at it carefully, not judging it but, rather, accepting and respecting it. Note the details of your creation. What do you see? Is there a part of it that your attention is drawn to? How does it feel to have completed it? What was the process of creating it like for you? What does it tell you about your life, if anything? Were you aware of any associations, memories, or connections as you were creating it? Congratulate yourself for having done it and give thanks.[12]

Live the Questions

Day after day, Deborah gently enters hospital rooms to hear the stories of patients and families. She is a loving resource to staff who balance caregiving with their own life demands. As a chaplain, Deborah has become an integral member of the healthcare team, offering her training, wisdom, and deep faith for those in crisis or facing challenges. Her commitment to ministry is also a commitment to living a full life, a life of hope. She speaks plainly about the path that brought her here. It has been a path of transformation, of entering the depths of her pain, and there discovering her God in the darkness of loss. Nearly forty years ago, Deborah's father was robbed and murdered.

Deborah grew up in a loving Jewish home. Following college, she stayed close to the ritual and prayer of her childhood as she built a new life with her husband and two children. A phone call from her hometown changed everything. With bereavement traditions at her side, Deborah moved forward in her life as best she could, her focus on her little girl and new son. But she was angry at God, and there she stayed for over ten years. The cruel injustice of this violent act robbed her of her father and betrayed her understanding of a loving God. Over time, she entered her anger and learned from it. She sought help through therapy, yoga, and meditation, and eventually returned to her practice of the Jewish tradition. She chose to remain conscious in her grief. No longer expecting the outside world to make her happy, she went inward to explore and savor her connection to love.

Deborah found the courage to seek help and understanding from others. Ultimately, she discovered the relationship with her father as a life-giving connection that now supports her work as a hospital chaplain. His lessons of compassion weave through their braid of love and are a part of Deborah's purpose in life. Her transformation continues and lives along-side her choices in life. Deborah's travels led her to the both/and of life, where loss and gratitude coexist, where hope and sadness touch.

Over a lifetime, we adapt and readapt to the losses in our lives. Hopefully, we can accept the mantle to grieve with con-sciousness and with self-compassion. But what comes next? What does a transformed life look like? Deborah's story renews our conversations about unitive thinking as a pathway for healing and transformation. Just as she learned to hold opposing emotions in her heart, we too are called to embrace the polarities of our grief experience. We are moving toward a blend of life's challenges and joys, with grief leading us forward. Richard G. Tedeschi and Lawrence G. Calhoun emphasize, "It is important to recognize that the transforma-tions of grief are essentially paradoxical."[13]

While *paradox* implies contradiction, it can also be seen as another entry into the discussion of the unitive mind. Once again, let the images of "both/and" support our understand-ing of grief and, in this case, paradox. Remember our study of the Dual Process Model of bereavement? It taught us that we move back and forth between the loss experience and the restoration experience of our grief. This pattern of oscillation guides us to one and then the other, teaching us to live in both places, *to live with paradox*. Tedeschi and Calhoun add, "Grieving involves taking action and tolerating inaction," yet another example of paradox in grief. It is so hard for most of us to sit still with our sadness, and yet we have learned that it is valuable. The unitive mind patiently teaches us to trust both places, where we experiment with moments of silent contem-plation *and* active expression of our feelings. Grief's paradox also appears in the wavering between needing support from others and choosing solitude for the very personal moments of loss. With time, we come to trust the back and forth of our needs. With self-compassion, we listen to the wisdom within that guides us toward companionship *and* toward privacy. The paradox of grieving trains our heart and mind and leads us through our own (as Tedeschi and Calhoun call it) "transformative struggle."

You are writing a new chapter of your life, one that incorporates the truth of your experience with the wisdom of your heart. As the meaning-maker, you shape the narrative as you go forward. You co-create with the Divine, gathering together new understandings, your loved one's blessings, and your own gifts that are waiting to be called upon. Your values and goals, sometimes revised through loss's lessons, set your boundaries. With a mature focus, you honor your inner life and all your hard work. Alan Wolfelt adds, "Every loss in life calls for a new search for meaning, including a natural struggle with spiritual concerns, often transforming your vision of God and your faith life."[14] As you go forward, know that the yearning that once seared your heart has been transformed into a call to savor life yet to be. Let your longing lead your heart.

This is the time to "nourish your transformed soul," Wolfelt reminds us. So much has transpired in your travels. He advises,

As you continue to experience how grief has transformed you, be open to the new directions your life is now taking. You have learned to watch for trail markers in your continued living. Listen to the wisdom of your inner voice. Make choices that are congruent with what you have learned on your journey.[15]

Soul nourishment comes in many forms:

• Time alone may become a new priority, for example, as you discover the benefits of contemplative practices.

- Volunteering at a soup kitchen or animal shelter may align with your transformed vision for your life.

- A regular "gratitude practice" may remind you of the blessings in your life.

- Nature's presence in your day may soothe aches and pains, offering moments of beauty.

- Music, and a responding bounce or wiggle, may fill your heart in all the right places.

- You may be led to support others who grieve, to join with, as Weller says, the "elders who have been seasoned by grief, recognizing we carry soul medicine for those who are beginning."[16]

Opportunities or relationships will come before you, inviting you to live authentically, rooted in the truth of who you are now. They are fruits of your labors in grief, reminders of the fullness of life.

Some of the relationships that have been with you throughout your journey may challenge your transformation. Friends and family members who shared your loss may respond to the loss differently than you do. Their journey, as yours, is unique to them. Their assumptive world has its own set of expectations. So as you continue to tend to yourself, there may be conflicts or disconnects with family and friends. You may feel impatient with or pull away from those you love as you negotiate these differences. As Robert A. Neimeyer carefully states,

> Ultimately, we are faced with the task of transforming our identities so as to redefine our symbolic connection to the deceased while maintaining our relationship with the living. Our attempts to do so may resonate or be dissonant with the views of others such as the immediate family.[17]

While this is normal, it can be challenging. Let your Land of Hope make room for such variations between you and others. If necessary, create space in these complicated relationships. Establish new boundaries, if needed. Let compassion be a part of your discernment—compassion for yourself and for others. Grief is ultimately a spiritual experience, and we are seekers. This life before you, this Land of Hope, is yours to shape and discover. As you move forward, embrace both the joys and the sorrows as part of the whole of your life. Love has seeped into your loss, soothed its ache, and released its grip. Your heart has been freed to love again, and the world around you is breathtaking. The sparrow's silhouette bounces up the roofline; the morning clouds float past your window; a gentle hum warms your home—and all invite you into *this moment*, where love holds you close. John E. Welshons reminds us, "To heal our grief, we must know that love is a state of being within us. It is not given to us by someone else. . . . When we 'fall in love' what we're really doing is touching the place within ourselves where *we are love*."[18]

Poet Rainer Maria Rilke offers tender encouragement for the path before us, for the new Land of Hope:

Have patience with everything that is unsolved in your heart and try to cherish the questions themselves, like closed rooms and like books written in a very strange tongue. Do not search now for the answers which cannot be given you because you could not live them. It is a matter of living everything. Live the questions now. Perhaps you will gradually, without noticing it, one distant day live right into the answer.[19]

You have learned that there are no clear solutions to life's demands on us. You have learned that the only way around your pain is through it. Let the wisdom you have gained guide you forward into new places, asking new questions. Let your heart remain open, even when there are no answers. This life before you may be unknown, but the love within you will sustain your journey.

Promptings of Hope

"For all that has been—Thanks. For all that shall be—Yes." One-time UN Secretary-General Dag Hammarskjold's words draw us into a simple acceptance of life. Simple and, at the same time, challenging for one who grieves. Your need for hope's presence will continue as life unfolds, so create a circle of love to support yourself on the journey.

Choose a quiet time and space, gather colored pencils and unlined paper, and take deep breaths to enter the moment more fully. This is sacred work and it deserves your full attention. Write your name in the center of the paper. Think of all the people who love you, including those who have passed away. Write each name in a large circle around your name, the "you" on that piece of paper. Write them slowly and mindfully. You may choose different colors or choose to add swirls or symbols in between the names. Let the process guide you.

After you write the names of family and close friends, allow your mind to go out into your life. The woman who taught you to knit, the neighbor who gave you a job when you were eight, that one teacher who "got" you. Each of them, in their own way, did indeed love you. They are all surrounding you, encouraging you, and loving you now as you move forward into your life. Try it. Claim the circle of love that is around you right now in the Land of Hope.

FINAL THOUGHTS

Books come to an end, but most people would say their grief will never end—it just changes. How do we bring this conversation to a close when you, dear reader, might be waiting for more, for the "one thing" that will ease your way once and for all? I hope that the images and ideas presented here have offered comfort and an alternative point of view as you navigate the changes within the Land of Loss. I hope you are becoming used to the idea that there is no solution other than grief itself. Not the grief you sought in order to erase the pain or speed things along, but the healing balm of grief that eases its way into your brokenness, calming the ache, lessening the sting. It seems our destiny as humans is to learn and return, learn and return, as we travel through life. T. S. Eliot reminds us,

> *What we call the beginning is often the end,*
> *And to make an end is to make a beginning.*
> *The end is where we start from.*[1]

The same is true for our grief. As we seek relief at the end of this journey, do we try to hide from the secret truth that a new beginning awaits, one without our loved one in it? Let's face this paradox of relief and sadness with hope in our heart. Our journey with grief has taught us the breadth and depth of love's legacy. I pray that our new beginnings are indeed filled with a renewed understanding of hope. Cynthia Bourgeault explains:

Hope's home is at the innermost point in us, and in all things. It is a quality of aliveness. It does not come at the end, as the feeling that results from a happy outcome. Rather, it lies at the beginning, as a pulse of truth that . . . will send us forth in hope, regardless of the physical circumstances of our lives. Hope fills us with the strength to stay present, to abide in the flow of the Mercy no matter what outer storms assail us. It is entered always and only through surrender; that is, through the willingness to let go of everything we are presently clinging to. And yet when we enter it, it enters *us* and fills us with its own life—a quiet strength beyond anything we have ever known.[2]

Such a hope is not reserved for saints. In fact, we who grieve are given that extra push into experiencing hope in our deepest places. Our surrender can lead us forward to where the Fountain of Hope has been all along. The fountain's reach is vast—perhaps you've felt the droplets a time or two along the way? In Alone and Passage, they appear as the possibility of a spring rain. You look around, hold out your hand to check. But no, the little drips and drops of water are just that, cool reminders of healing rains to come. In the Land of Loss, the droplets come from a fountain just out of sight, and they are a gift. When you feel the cool taps on your head, you might remember yourself as happy, and believe, if only for an instant, that happiness and loss can coexist. You might receive hope's wet kiss while at prayer, with the slightest but very real experience of love returning to your heart. Perhaps the fountain's spray comes disguised as your tears, which could mean more than a few wet reminders of hope. How blessed you are, for as your heart opens to your grief it is learning to abide in hope's flow of mercy and love. If you feel these droplets, take time to recognize or even name them. Let these gifts enfranchise your grief as you move forward, sustaining you as you enter Surrender. Know that the fullness of hope awaits and will boost your courage at the Cliffs of Uncertainty. Look around and receive support from all the sojourners, grievers, and others who seek a deeper relationship with hope. Perhaps you have seen rainbow colors thrown out by the fountain's mists. These are reminders of covenant and new life, revealed through the prism of hope's healing waters.

If you have imagined the Land of Loss with me as we have made our way through Alone and Passage, and perhaps Surrender and Changed, I hope you have found comfort in hearing stories of those who know these paths. Oftentimes, the unique experience of our grief magnifies the extreme loneliness and isolation we are feeling. We begin to question ourselves, upset that we are not handling our grief very well or wondering if we are abnormal in our reaction to loss. Be assured, the stories are inspired by real people with real reactions to the unpredictable demands of loss. Each region in this land has its own set of landmarks, its own rhythm. Those who travel through sometimes add their own signposts to help point the way, especially when it feels as if they are going in circles. I hope you too have learned to trust your instincts, and added stone towers or wooden arrows on your path to keep track of where you are and where you are going. It is your Land of Loss, your experience to decipher.

It has been a gift to me to share these thoughts with you. My passion to share images and insight to support your healing has led me back through my own Land of Loss with a renewed understanding. I am grateful for that and for the new lessons I have learned. If something has been helpful for you, I am so glad. If not, please just let it go. As a familiar idiom reminds us, we can separate the wheat from the chaff to discover the best resource for our nourishment. Trust your personal wisdom as you discern the best path. If this effort has not been helpful, please keep looking. Your heart's call for healing will guide you if you ask and listen. Please know that prayers for continued healing are coming your way. Healing from loss has the potential to lead you back to the core of your truest self, the "you" that your loved one knew and loved . . . to the place where love is born. T. S. Eliot continues,

> *We shall not cease from exploration,*
> *And the end of all our exploring*
> *Will be to arrive where we started*
> *And know the place for the first time.*[3]

ACKNOWLEDGMENTS

A book is shaped by the lives we lead and the people in them. I have been blessed by friends and family that love me and support my efforts to share what I have learned. I gratefully acknowledge the Mercy community and it's welcoming heart; those brave souls that shared their stories with me through the Hospital of Saint Raphael's bereavement program; my sons' dear presence in my life; and my husband's steadfast love throughout this process. My grateful heart sings.

NOTES

INTRODUCTION

1. Alan D. Wolfelt, "The Mourner's Bill of Rights," Center for Loss and Life Transition. Reprinted with permission from "The Mourner's Bill of Rights" by Alan D. Wolfelt, PhD.

2. Alan D. Wolfelt, *Understanding Your Grief: Ten Essential Touchstones for Finding Hope and Healing Your Heart* (Fort Collins, CO: Companion Press, 2003), 3. Reprinted with permission by Alan D. Wolfelt, PhD.

3. Rainer Maria Rilke, *Sonnets to Orpheus*, part 2, sonnet 29 , in *In Praise of Mortality: Selections from Rainer Maria Rilke's* Duino Elegies *and* Sonnets to Orpheus, translated and edited by Anita Barrows and Joanna Macy (New York: Riverhead, 2005), 135.

PART 1: ALONE

1. George Bonanno, *The Other Side of Sadness: What the New Science of Bereavement Tells Us about Life after Loss* (New York: Basic Books, 2009), 6.

2. Ibid., 7.

CHAPTER 1: ENTERING LOSS

1. John E. Welshons, *Awakening from Grief: Finding the Way Back to Joy*, 2003. Reprinted with permission of New World Library, Novato, CA. www.newworldlibrary.com, 2.

2. Ibid.

3. J. William Worden, *Grief Counseling and Grief Therapy: A Handbook for the Mental Health Practitioner*, 4th ed. (New York: Springer, 2009), 39.

4. Ibid., 42.

5. Joan Didion, *The Year of Magical Thinking* (New York: Vintage, 2007), 188.

6. Barbara Lazear Ascher, "A Widow's First Five Years," *Town and Country* (July 2007): 113–14. Available at www. barbaralazearascher.com/images/essays/grief/widowfirstfive.pdf.

7. Paul C. Rosenblatt, "Grief That Does Not End," in *Continuing Bonds: New Understandings of Grief*, edited by Dennis Klass, Phyllis R. Silverman, and Steven L. Nickman (Washington, DC: Taylor and Francis, 1996), 50.

8. Francis Weller, *The Wild Edge of Sorrow: Rituals of Renewal and the Sacred Work of Grief* (Berkeley, CA: North Atlantic Books, 2015), xix.

9. Ibid.

10. Barbara Lazear Ascher, *Landscape without Gravity: A Memoir of Grief* (New York: Penguin, 1994).

11. Brené Brown, *Daring Greatly: How the Courage to Be Vulnerable Transforms the Way We Live, Love, Parent and Lead* (New York: Avery, 2015), 33.

12. Ibid.

13. Jalal al-Din Rumi, *The Essential Rumi*, translated by Coleman Barks (New York: HarperCollins, 1995), 109.

14. Brown, *Daring Greatly*, 34.

15. Thomas Attig, *How We Grieve: Relearning the World* (New York: Oxford University Press, 1996), 19.

16. Therese A. Rando, *How to Go On Living When Someone You Love Dies* (Lexington, MA: Lexington Books, 1988), 25.

17. Jaqueline Weaver, "Study Finds That Yearning—Not Disbelief—Is Defining Feature of Grief," *Yale Bulletin and Calendar* 35, no. 21 (March 9, 2007), http://archives.news.yale.edu/v35.n21/story16.html.

18. Attig, *How We Grieve*, 39.

19. Alan D. Wolfelt, *Understanding Your Grief: Ten Essential Touchstones for Finding Hope and Healing Your Heart* (Fort Collins, CO: Companion Press, 2003), 70. Reprinted with permission by Alan D. Wolfelt, PhD.

20. Rando, *How to Go On Living*, 45.

21. Wolfelt, *Understanding Your Grief*, 106.

22. Attig, *How We Grieve*, 16.

23. Robert A. Neimeyer, *Lessons of Loss: A Guide to Coping* (Memphis: Center for the Study of Loss and Transition, 2000), 92.

24. Ibid., 93.

Chapter 2: Gathering Your Resources

1. Francis Weller, *The Wild Edge of Sorrow: Rituals of Renewal and the Sacred Work of Grief* (Berkeley, CA: North Atlantic Books, 2015), 14.

2. Alexander H. Jordan and Brett T. Litz, "Prolonged Grief Disorder: Diagnostic, Assessment, and Treatment Considerations," *Professional Psychology: Research and Practice* 45, no. 3 (2014): 180–87, www.apa.org/pubs/journals/features /pro-a0036836.pdf.

3. Colin Murray Parkes, "Complicated Grief: The Debate over a New DSM-V Diagnostic Category," in *Living with Grief: Before and after the Death*, edited by Kenneth Doka (Washington, DC: Hospice Foundation of America, 2007), 142.

4. Thomas Attig, *How We Grieve: Relearning the World* (New York: Oxford University Press, 1996), 122.

5. Daniel Goleman, "Mourning: New Studies Affirm Its Benefits," *New York Times* (February 5, 1985), www.nytimes.com/1985/02/05 /science/mourning-new-studies-affirm-its-benefits.html.

6. Alan D. Wolfelt, *Understanding Your Grief: Ten Essential Touchstones for Finding Hope and Healing Your Heart* (Fort Collins, CO: Companion Press, 2003), 12. Reprinted with permission by Alan D. Wolfelt, PhD.

7. Ibid.

8. Weller, *The Wild Edge of Sorrow*, 24.

9. Arthur Powell Davies, "Of Joy and Sorrow" (sermon), reprinted in *The Faith of an Unrepentant Liberal* (Boston: Beacon Press, 1947), 109.

10. Richard Rohr, *The Naked Now: Learning to See as the Mystics See* (New York: Crossroad, 2009), 32.

11. Ibid., 123.

Chapter 3: Unexpected Landmarks and Land Mines

1. Tory Zellick, "Shoulda, Coulda, Woulda: Dealing with Grief and Guilt after a Loved One Passes," Huffington Post (March 20, 2013), www.huffingtonpost.com/tory-zellick/should-coulda-woulda-deal_b_2497327.html.

2. Therese A. Rando, *How to Go on Living When Someone You Love Dies* (Lexington, MA: Lexington Books, 1988), 35.

3. Darin Strauss, *Half a Life: A Memoir* (New York: Random House, 2011), 4.

4. Stephen Levine, *Unattended Sorrow: Recovering from Loss and Reviving the Heart* (Emmaus, PA: Rodale Books, 2005), 101.

5. Ibid.

6. Ashley Davis Bush, *Transcending Loss: Understanding the Lifelong Impact of Grief and How to Make It Meaningful* (New York: Berkley, 1997), 22.

7. George A. Bonanno, *The Other Side of Sadness: What the New Science of Bereavement Tells Us about Life after Loss* (New York: Basic Books, 2009), 35.

8. Ibid.

PART 2: PASSAGE

1. J. William Worden, *Grief Counseling and Grief Therapy: A Handbook for the Mental Health Practitioner*, 4th ed. (New York: Springer, 2009), 44.

CHAPTER 4: CHALLENGES AND CHANGES TO YOUR IDENTITY

1. Robert A. Neimeyer, "The Life Imprint," in *Techniques of Grief Therapy: Creative Practices for Counseling the Bereaved*, edited by Robert A. Neimeyer (New York: Routledge, 2012), 274.

2. Thomas Attig, *How We Grieve: Relearning the World* (New York: Oxford University Press, 1996), 158.

3. Barbara Lazear Ascher, *Landscape without Gravity: A Memoir of Grief* (New York: Penguin Books, 1993), 47.

4. Abraham Twerski, *A Formula for Proper Living: Practical Lessons from Life and Torah* (Woodstock, VT: Jewish Lights, 2009), 89.

5. Alan D. Wolfelt, *Understanding Your Grief: Ten Essential Touchstones for Finding Hope and Healing Your Heart* (Fort Collins, CO: Companion Press, 2003), 94. Reprinted with permission by Alan D. Wolfelt, PhD.

6. Francis Weller, *The Wild Edge of Sorrow: Rituals of Renewal and the Sacred Work of Grief* (Berkeley, CA: North Atlantic Books, 2015), 151.

7. Ibid., 152.

8. Vicki Panagotacos, "Defining and Envisioning Self," in *Techniques of Grief Therapy: Creative Practices for Counseling the Bereaved*, edited by Robert A. Neimeyer (New York: Routledge, 2012), 292.

9. Attig, *How We Grieve*, 147.

10. Cynthia Lynn Wall, *The Courage to Trust: A Guide to Building Deep and Lasting Relationships* (Oakland, CA: New Harbinger, 2004), 12.

11. Ibid., 13.

CHAPTER 5: OUR GUIDES AND OUR GATEKEEPERS

1. C. S. Lewis, *A Grief Observed* (Grand Rapids, MI: Zondervan, 1989), 71.

2. Charles A. Corr, "Revisiting the Concept of Disenfranchised Grief," in *Disenfranchised Grief: New Directions, Challenges, and Strategies for Practice*, edited by Kenneth Doka (Champaign, IL: Research Press, 2001), 51.

3. Margaret Mead, "Ritual and Social Crisis," in *The Roots of Ritual*, edited by J. D. Shaughnessy (Grand Rapids, MI: Eerdmans, 1973), 89.

4. Kathleen R. Gilbert and Gloria D. Horsley, "Technology and Grief Support in the Twenty-First Century: A Multimedia Platform," in *Grief and Bereavement in Contemporary Society: Bridging Research and Practice*, edited by Robert A. Neimeyer, et al. (New York: Routledge, 2011), 368.

5. Taya Dunn, "Grieving in the Technology Age Is Uncharted Territory," Upworthy.com, July 20, 2016, www.upworthy.com /please-read-this-before-you-post-another-rip-on-social-media.

6. William James, "Confidences of a Psychical Researcher," *The American Magazine* 68 (1909): 589.

7. Doka, *Disenfranchised Grief*, 5.

8. Charles A. Corr, "Revisiting the Concept of Disenfranchised Grief," in *Disenfranchised Grief*, 52.

9. Therese A. Rando, *How to Go On Living When Someone You Love Dies* (Lexington, MA: Lexington Books, 1988), 57.

CHAPTER 6: CREATING YOUR OWN MAP

1. Kenneth R. Mitchell and Herbert Anderson, *All Our Losses, All Our Griefs: Resources for Pastoral Care* (Philadelphia: Westminster Press, 1983), 83.

2. George Bonanno, *The Other Side of Sadness: What the New Science of Bereavement Tells Us about Life after Loss* (New York: Basic Books, 2009), 40.

3. Margaret Stroebe and Henk Schut, "The Dual Process Model of Coping with Bereavement: A Decade On," *OMEGA: Journal of Death and Dying* 61, no. 4 (2010): 273–89.

4. Cynthia L. Schultz and Darcy L. Harris, "Giving Voice to Nonfinite Loss and Grief in Bereavement," in *Grief and Bereavement in Contemporary Society: Bridging Research and Practice*, edited by Robert A. Neimeyer et al. (New York: Routledge, 2011), 241.

5. Hara Estroff Marano, "The Art of Resilience," *Psychology Today* (May 1, 2003), www.psychologytoday.com/articles/200305/the-art-resilience.

6. Bonanno, *The Other Side of Sadness*, 81.

7. Linda Graham, *Bouncing Back: Rewiring Your Brain for Maximum Resilience and Well-Being* (Novato: CA, New World Library, 2013), xxv.

8. Compiled from Linda Graham, "Neuroscience and the Art of Self Care," Psychotherapy Networker Symposium, Washington, DC, March 22, 2012, workshop handout. Available at http://lindagraham-mft.net/wp-content/uploads/2012/04/3-16-12_Neuroscience_and_the_Art_of_Self_Care.pdf.

PART 3: SURRENDER

1. Henri J. M. Nouwen, *The Only Necessary Thing: Living a Prayerful Life* (New York: Crossroad, 2008).

2. Francis Weller, *The Wild Edge of Sorrow: Rituals of Renewal and the Sacred Work of Grief* (Berkeley, CA: North Atlantic Books, 2015), 5.

3. Doris Klein, *Journey of the Soul* (Franklin, WI: Sheed and Ward, 2000), 112.

CHAPTER 7: A COURAGEOUS CHOICE

1. Alan D. Wolfelt, *Understanding Your Grief: Ten Essential Touchstones for Finding Hope and Healing Your Heart* (Fort Collins, CO: Companion Press, 2003), 2. Reprinted with permission by Alan D. Wolfelt, PhD.

2. Miriam Greenspan, *Healing through the Dark Emotions: The Wisdom of Grief, Fear, and Despair* (Boston: Shambhala, 2003), 2. Reprinted by arrangement with Shambhala Publications, Inc., Boulder, CO., www.shambhala.com.

3. Elie Kaplan Spitz, *Healing from Despair: Choosing Wholeness in a Broken World* (Woodstock, VT: Jewish Lights, 2010), 41.

4. Greenspan, *Healing through the Dark Emotions*, 42.

5. J. William Worden, *Grief Counseling and Grief Therapy: A Handbook for the Mental Health Practitioner*, 2nd ed. (New York: Springer, 1991), 48.

6. Greenspan, *Healing through the Dark Emotions*, 12.

7. Brené Brown, *The Gifts of Imperfection: Let Go of Who You Think You're Supposed to Be and Embrace Who You Are* (Center City, MN: Hazelden, 2010), 6.

8. Osho, *Courage: The Joy of Living Dangerously* (New York: St Martin's, 1999), 6.

9. Heather Stang, *Mindfulness and Grief: With Guided Meditations to Calm Your Mind and Restore Your Spirit* (London: CICO Books, 2014), 14.

10. "First Three Steps of AA Define the Problem, Solution," Hazelden Betty Ford Foundation, www.hazelden.org/web/public/has90524.page.

11. *Alcoholics Anonymous: The Story of How Many Thousands of Men and Women Have Recovered from Alcoholism* (New York: Alcoholics Anonymous World Services, 2001), 59.

12. Wayne Edward Oates, *Your Particular Grief* (Philadelphia: Westminster, 1981), 111.

13. Rami M. Shapiro, *Recovery—the Sacred Art: The Twelve Steps as Spiritual Practice* (Woodstock, VT: SkyLight Paths, 2009), 18.

14. Greenspan, *Healing through the Dark Emotions*, 40.

15. Ibid.

16. Shapiro, *Recovery—the Sacred Art*, 43.

17. John E. Welshons, *Awakening from Grief: Finding the Way Back to Joy*, 2003. Reprinted with permission of New World Library, Novato, CA. www.newworldlibrary.com, 88.

18. Ibid.

19. Jeannie Ewing, *From Grief to Grace: The Journey from Tragedy to Triumph* (Manchester, NH: Sophia Institute Press, 2016), 78.

20. Shapiro, *Recovery—the Sacred Art*, 41.

21. *Twelve Steps and Twelve Traditions* (New York: Alcoholics Anonymous World Services, 2005), 36.

22. Marya Hornbacher, *Waiting: A Nonbeliever's Higher Power* (Center City, MN: Hazelden, 2011), xiii.

23. Ibid., xiv.

24. Ibid., xix.

Chapter 8: Letting Go into Love

1. Doris Klein, *Journey of the Soul* (Franklin, WI: Sheed and Ward, 2000), 92.

2. Francis Weller, *The Wild Edge of Sorrow: Rituals of Renewal and the Sacred Work of Grief* (Berkeley, CA: North Atlantic Books, 2015), 122.

3. Dennis Klass, "Inner Reality and Social Reality: Bonds with Dead Children and the Resolution of Grief," in *Living with Grief: Before and after the Death*, edited by Kenneth Doka (Washington, DC: Hospice Foundation of America, 2007), 234.

4. Cynthia Bourgeault, *The Wisdom Jesus: Transforming Heart and Mind—a New Perspective on Christ and His Message* (Boston: Shambhala, 2008), 43. Reprinted by arrangement with Shambhala Publications, Inc., Boulder, CO. www.shambhala.com.

5. Ibid.

6. Richard G. Tedeschi and Lawrence G. Calhoun, "Grief as a Transformative Struggle," in *Living with Grief*, 115.

7. Stephen Levine, *Unattended Sorrow: Recovering from Loss and Reviving the Heart* (Emmaus, PA: Rodale, 2005), 127.

8. Thomas Attig, *How We Grieve: Relearning the World* (New York: Oxford University Press, 1996),175.

9. Ibid., 176.

10. Ilia Delio, *The Humility of God: A Franciscan Perspective* (Cincinnati: Franciscan Media, 2005), 23.

11. Jan Richardson, *The Cure for Sorrow: A Book of Blessings for Times of Grief* (Orlando, FL: Wanton Godspeller Press, 2016), xv. www.janrichardson.com

12. Alan D. Wolfelt, *Understanding Your Grief: Ten Essential Touchstones for Finding Hope and Healing Your Heart* (Fort Collins, CO: Companion Press, 2003), 3. Reprinted with permission by Alan D. Wolfelt, PhD.

13. Levine, *Unattended Sorrow*, 221.

14. Christine Valters Paintner, *Eyes of the Heart: Photography as a Christian Contemplative Practice* (Notre Dame, IN: Sorin Books, 2013), 30.

15. Wolfelt, *Understanding Your Grief*, 4.

16. Betsy Caprio and Thomas M. Hedberg, *Coming Home: A Handbook for Exploring the Sanctuary Within* (Mahwah, NJ: Paulist Press, 1986), 215.

17. Joyce Rupp, *Praying Our Goodbyes* (Notre Dame, IN: Ave Maria Press, 1988), 109.

18. John E. Welshons, *Awakening from Grief: Finding the Way Back to Joy*, 2003. Reprinted with permission of New World Library, Novato, CA. www.newworldlibrary.com, 93.

19. Stephen Levine, *Healing into Life and Death* (New York: Anchor Books, 1987), 108.

20. Adapted from Gina Barreca, "An Emotional Rescue in the Dark Night of the Soul," *Hartford Courant* (August 6, 2001), http://articles.courant.com/2001-08-06/features/0108060301_1_nightmares-demons-dark-night.

21. Weller, *The Wild Edge of Sorrow*, 151.

22. Bourgeault, *The Wisdom Jesus*, 45.

23. Klein, *Journey of the Soul*, 87.

24. Weller, *The Wild Edge of Sorrow*, 155.

25. Ibid., 154.

26. Klein, *Journey of the Soul*, 88.

27. Richardson, *The Cure for Sorrow*, 78.

Part 4: Changed

1. Joyce Rupp, *Praying Our Goodbyes* (Notre Dame, IN: Ave Maria Press, 1988), 101.

2. Alan D. Wolfelt, *Understanding Your Grief: Ten Essential Touchstones for Finding Hope and Healing Your Heart* (Fort Collins, CO: Companion Press, 2003), 153. Reprinted with permission by Alan D. Wolfelt, PhD.

Chapter 9: Contemplate a New Horizon

1. Joyce Rupp, *Praying Our Goodbyes* (Notre Dame, IN: Ave Maria Press, 1988), 100.

2. Francis Weller, *The Wild Edge of Sorrow: Rituals of Renewal and the Sacred Work of Grief* (Berkeley, CA: North Atlantic Books, 2015), 101.

3. Alan D. Wolfelt, *Understanding Your Grief: Ten Essential Touchstones for Finding Hope and Healing Your Heart* (Fort Collins, CO: Companion Press, 2003), 158.

4. Robert A. Emmons, *Thanks! How Practicing Gratitude Can Make You Happier* (New York: Houghton Mifflin Harcourt, 2007), 6.

5. David Steindl-Rast, *Gratefulness, the Heart of Prayer: An Approach to Life in Fullness* (New York: Paulist Press, 1984), 12.

6. Ibid., 15–16.

7. Ibid., 17.

8. Gertrud Mueller Nelson, *To Dance with God: Family Ritual and Community Celebration* (New York: Paulist Press, 1986), 25.

9. Tania Brocklehurst, "Read: Interview with Robert Neimeyer by Tania," BereavementUK, September 5, 2015, http://www.bereavement.co.uk/Media-Centre/?p=1214.

10. Therese A. Rando, *How to Go On Living When Someone You Love Dies* (Lexington, MA: Lexington Books, 1988), 261.

11. Ibid., 262.

12. Weller, *The Wild Edge of Sorrow*, 76.

13. George Bonanno, *The Other Side of Sadness: What the New Science of Bereavement Tells Us about Life after Loss* (New York: Basic Books, 2009), 192.

14. Ibid.

15. Ibid., 191.
16. Rando, *How to Go On Living*, 265.
17. Nelson, *To Dance with God*, 34.
18. Weller, *The Wild Edge of Sorrow*, 80.
19. Rando, *How to Go On Living*, 263.
20. Ibid.
21. Ibid., 264.
22. Ibid., 262.
23. Alice Parsons Zulli, "Healing Rituals: Powerful and Empowering," in *Living with Grief: Who We Are, How We Grieve*, edited by Kenneth J. Doka and Joyce D. Davidson (Washington, DC: Hospice Foundation of America, 1998), 261.

CHAPTER 10: LAND OF HOPE

1. Stephen Levine, *Unattended Sorrow: Recovering from Loss and Reviving the Heart* (Emmaus, PA: Rodale, 2005), 218.
2. Václav Havel, *Disturbing the Peace* (New York: Random House, 1991), 181.
3. Phyllis R. Silverman and Dennis Klass, "Introduction: What's the Problem?" in *Continuing Bonds: New Understandings of Grief*, edited by Dennis Klass, Phyllis R. Silverman, and Steven L. Nickman (Washington, DC: Taylor and Francis, 1996), 5.
4. Margaret Stroebe, Mary Gergen, Kenneth Gergen, and Wolfgang Stroebe, "Broken Hearts or Broken Bonds?" in *Continuing Bonds*, 32.
5. George A. Bonanno, *The Other Side of Sadness: What the New Science of Bereavement Tells Us about Life after Loss* (New York: Basic Books, 2009), 201.
6. J. William Worden, *Grief Counseling and Grief Therapy: A Handbook for the Mental Health Practitioner*, 4th ed. (New York: Springer, 2009), 51.
7. Bonanno, *The Other Side of Sadness*, 142.
8. Thomas Attig, *How We Grieve: Relearning the World* (New York: Oxford University Press, 1996), 176.
9. Ibid., 188.
10. Ibid., 175.

11. *Mishkan T'filah: Services for Shabbat; A Reform Siddur*, edited by Elyse D. Frishman (New York: Central Conference of American Rabbis, 2007), 291.

12. Rose Amodeo Petronella, *Honoring the Soul: Mandalas for Inspiration and Insight* (Middletown, CT: www.lulu.com, 2015), 64–5.

13. Richard G. Tedeschi and Lawrence G. Calhoun, "Grief as a Transformative Struggle," in *Living with Grief: Before and after the Death*, edited by Kenneth J. Doka (Washington, DC: Hospice Foundation of America, 2007), 107.

14. Alan D. Wolfelt, *Understanding Your Grief: Ten Essential Touchstones for Finding Hope and Healing Your Heart* (Fort Collins, CO: Companion Press, 2003), 156. Reprinted with permission by Alan D. Wolfelt, PhD.

15. Ibid., 161.

16. Francis Weller, *The Wild Edge of Sorrow: Rituals of Renewal and the Sacred Work of Grief* (Berkeley, CA: North Atlantic Books, 2015), 144.

17. Robert A. Neimeyer, *Lessons of Loss: A Guide to Coping* (Memphis: Center for the Study of Loss and Transition, 2000), 98.

18. John E. Welshons, *Awakening from Grief: Finding the Way Back to Joy*, 2003. Reprinted with permission of New World Library, Novato, CA. www.newworldlibrary.com, 136.

19. Rainer Maria Rilke, *Letters to a Young Poet* (La Vergne, TN: BN Publishing, 2008), 21.

FINAL THOUGHTS

1. T. S. Eliot, "Little Gidding," in *Four Quartets* (New York: Houghton Mifflin Harcourt, 2014), 58.

2. Cynthia Bourgeault, *Mystical Hope: Trusting in the Mercy of God* (Lanham, MD: Rowman & Littlefield, 2001), 87.

3. Eliot, *Four Quartets*, 59.

SUGGESTIONS FOR
FURTHER READING

Brene Brown. *The Gift of Imperfection: Let Go of Who You Think You're Supposed to Be and Embrace Who You Ar*. Center City, MN: Hazelden, 2010.

George Bonnano. *The Other Side of Sadness: What the New Science of Bereavement Tells Us about Life after Loss*. New York: Basic Books, 2009.

Joan Didion. *The Year of Magical Thinking*. New York: Knopf Books, 2005.

Jeannie Ewing. *From Grief to Grace: The Journey from Tragedy to Triumph*. Manchester, NH: Sophia Institute Press, 2016.

C.S. Lewis. *A Grief Observed*. New York: HarperOne, 2001.

Joyce Rupp. *Praying Our Goodbyes*. Notre Dame, IN: Ave Maria Press, 1988.

Heather Stang. *Mindfulness and Grief: With Guided meditations to Calm Your Mind and Restore Your Spirit*. London: CICO Books, 2014.

Francis Weller. *The Wild Edge of Sorrow: Rituals of Renewal and the Sacred Work of Grief*. Berkeley, CA: North Atlantic Books, 2015.

Alan Wolfelt. *Understanding Your Grief: Ten Essential Touchstones for Finding Hope and Healing Your Heart*. Fort Collins, CO: Companion Press, 2003.